SPRING 49

A JOURNAL OF

ARCHETYPE

AND

CULTURE

1989

SPRING PUBLICATIONS
P.O. Box 222069
Dallas, Texas 75222

CONTENTS

III. Heavy-Duty

IV. Worthwhile

V. Contributors

ACKNOWLEDGMENTS

To Princeton University Press for quotations from the *Collected Works* *(CW)* of C.G. Jung (Bollingen Series XX), translated by R.F.C. Hull, edited by H. Read, M. Fordham, G. Adler, and Wm. McGuire, and published in Great Britain by Routledge and Kegan Paul, London. Other quotations have been acknowledged throughout in appropriate notes and references.

Spring 1989 is edited by James Hillman, Charles Boer, and Ross Miller, assisted by Mary Helen Sullivan, Jay Livernois, and Eric Purchase.

AMERICAN INDIAN HUMORS

KENNETH LINCOLN

Back Home

I had read *Black Elk Speaks* by the end of the 1960s—a strangely troubling, still visionary story about my Northern Plains home. A Japanese friend in graduate school lent me a new novel, *House Made of Dawn,* by a Kiowa writer as yet unknown (Momaday's Pulitzer was a few months away). Then in spring 1969 *Playboy* published Vine Deloria's piece "Anthropologists and Other Friends," from the outrageously titled *Custer Died for Your Sins* (originally a bumper sticker to goad missionaries). The essay was illustrated by a casually dressed, contemporary Indian pinned in a specimen box. I read it in the city engineer's drafting room where I worked vacations in Alliance, Nebraska, to attend college.

Deloria's essay on Indians was hilarious! A Standing Rock Sioux who published in *Playboy*! In Alliance rednecks didn't consider Indians funny, and hardly literate; my callow stereotypes shattered.

Little did I know of Scott Momaday's finely resonant sense of humor (in a month he would buy me a hamburger on Berkeley's Telegraph Avenue). Nor did I know that Nick Black Elk had been a sacred Sioux clown around my own hometown, along with Joe Chips. And I discovered that Vine Deloria, Jr., was not only a budding lawyer and skilled writer, but a Lutheran divinity student for four years. Here he was publishing in a best-selling magazine *on Indian humor*! I had a few things to learn.

Indians do laugh a lot. The most engaging minds I've known—Al Logan Slagle, Mark Monroe, Paula Gunn Allen, Alfonso Ortiz, Vee Salabiye, Vine Deloria, Duane Champagne, Hanay Geiogamah, Mike Kabotie, Barney Bush, Harry Fonseca, Rebecca Tsosie—laugh the heartiest. The Lone Wolf and Monroe families from Pine Ridge and Rosebud, now Alliance (and now many more surnames with more families), took me in as kinsman to share their hurt and humor—Grandpa "Buffalo" Bill, the irrepressible George Lone Wolf (our local *heyoka*), the two Connies, Butch, Mark, and all the clansmen and kids. The Sioux medicine men in my life, Dawson No Horse, John Fire, Lawrence Antoine, were some of the wisest stand-up clowns I've known. Jenny Lone Wolf, who lived through her eighties as a family healer in Alliance, Nebraska, was a quietly powerful humorist of my hometown. She gave me some good reasons to laugh at myself and with her many families. Like her "took in" grandson, Sonny Boy, I was encouraged to feel at home, despite my non-Indian handicap. Aside from domestic humor—kitchen to back porch—the tribal "cement" of the Pan-Indian movement today, Deloria says, comes through Indian humor. "When people can laugh at themselves and laugh at others and hold all aspects of life together without letting anybody drive them to extremes, then it seems to me that that people can survive" (*Custer,* 167). This humor is both traditional and contemporary, trickster and geo-political.

Not only do Indians bond and revitalize, scapegoat and survive through laughter, but also they draw on millennia-old traditions of Trickster gods and holy fools, comic romance and epic boast. There is, and always has been, humor among Indians—and some five hundred tribal variants of such in the contiguous United States, locally indigenous to climate and geography, genetics and history. While "The" Trickster is pan-Indian, and some forms of libidinous humor surface in all tribal creation myths, from African *Ananse* to Chinese Monkey King, *Wichikapache* is specifically a Cree fool of the North who teaches survival through error. *Wakdjunkaga*, a near relative, breaks all the Winnebago rules to prove them. Pueblo *koshaves* in the Southwest drink urine and bathe in dung to stretch the limits of the gods, inversely to relieve ceremonial tension (these spirits have no human boundaries). The Iroquois false-face creator in the Northeast illustrates the doublings of reality, true and false twin, and the Navajo *Ma'ii*, or Coyote Old Man, both helps to recreate the Southwest as "first-born" of male and female creators *and* to rearrange or decreate it a bit. Always messing around, he is a comic "changing" spirit who continues the shape changings, just as the Mother Earth herself, Changing Woman, rejuvenates a cyclical world "with grace and beauty." So goes the ideal formula for aging among the Navajo.

The particularities here are not easy to assimilate for non-Indians, steeped in the American work ethic, plain moral styles, and a Puritan exclusion of humor from serious or sacred sites (as I grew up, anyway), and specifics are not exactly intertribal. Navajo and Sioux and Hopi and Crow and Chippewa aren't much unified on anything but resistance to Anglo encroachment, as Deloria notes the high frequency of jokes about Columbus and Custer. Still, this study focuses on the ethnic glue of Indian humor, a common denominator with culture-specific facets. Some of the broader continuities and overlaps should dispel an anti-myth, that Indians have no humor or linguistic subtlety. The tribal specifics of cases over time and terrain indicate just the opposite. Indians laugh with a special significance among themselves—from the traditional Blackfeet Dung Suitor to Jim Welch's farting horse in *Winter in the Blood*, from puckish jumping mice, to shifty-eyed ravens, to pigeon-toed coyotes, all the way to Louise Erdrich's lyric feminist humor in modern fiction and Momaday's wise-cracking peyote priest Tosamah in *House Made of Dawn* (the author's own alter-ego in the recesses of Los Angeles). To unify, to purge, to regenerate, Northrop Frye says in *Anatomy of Criticism*, enact the muses of spring, the three fates of the comic spirit. These remain particularly *native* to America, Indian in origin, if not universal to mankind. "One of the best ways to understand a people,"

Deloria writes, "is to know what makes them laugh" (*Custer*, 146). Indian humor may well be the undiscovered index, as yet, to America's first peoples.

Constance Rourke finds our national character in a distinctly "American" humor (*American Humor*, 1931, the year Neihardt heard Black Elk speak). American humor taps resilient and liberated resources, a frontier or liminal courage to face "west" toward the uncharted, the wild, the Indian America—tropes of mystery and rich origin. Out West, Vine Deloria's premises in *Custer Died for Your Sins* anticipate the audacity (and Red humor) of his second tract, the claim that our native *God Is Red* (1973). Deloria's own work and life present American native proof that law, religion, literature, social science, and comedy *can* have a common axis in Indian humor—an integrative spirit from Indian America (and reach a general reading public outside academia, to wit, *Playboy*). Deloria writes and thinks with the best of quick-shot, trick-riding marksmen. The art of his native humor provides telling examples of Freud's "economy" of release in dreams, jokes, and poetry. "What did you call this country before Columbus?" the Indian buff asks. "Ours."

A submerged, then "released" comic voice here expresses the collective set of "the people" and speaks for tribal, regional, and national psyches. Americans-at-large these days are looking, as they have long searched, for "what" to call this country: is it finally "ours"? And Deloria's Red wit is honed by a *human* science, law not the least, no-nonsense, honest, engaging. Real things are at stake, cultural and self-definitional at the heart of matters (Huizinga will call this *agon* of all "play")—all this can be tapped, if not indeed measured, in Indian humor.

"Let us examine the facts," Corn Tassel in 1785 addressed "brother warriors" of Whites who came to treat with Cherokees "at the forest's edge" for peace (and land). Having invaded in the dead of night and driven the tribes into the woods, now the Whites come to "talk of the law of nature and the law of nations, and they are both against you," Corn Tassel admonishes ironically (Peter Nabokov, *Native American Testimony*, 153–55: this collection, as a whole, best illustrates the range of Indian oratory "at the forest's edge," though a reader could draw from several dozen others). Whites arrogantly insist, Corn Tassel continues, that Indians "adopt your laws, your religion, your manners and customs," but the Cherokee consider the "good effect of these doctrines," if any, rather than "hearing you talk about them, or reading your papers." Talk's cheap, he says with sweet reason and no small ironic twist. We already have law, religion, manners, and customs; it's what makes us Cherokee. Whites want Indians to farm as they do. "May we not, with equal propriety, ask, why the white people do not hunt and live as we do?" Corn Tassel's contrary inversion carries the comic appeal of plain talk and true dialogue: we are *not* "your slaves. *We are a separate people!*" Indian nations are free-standing—Alfonso Ortiz insists still today, always so—and "treated" by the United States nominally as "sovereign" nations. The "great God of Nature" has placed two peoples "in different situations," Corn Tassel says. The best treaty here would be drawn from a co-existent cultural tolerance, the worst a tragic xenophobia. Nature has stocked White lands "with cows, ours with buffalo; yours with hog, ours with bear; yours with sheep, ours with deer." This God has given Whites the "advantage," Corn Tassel concedes wryly, since "your cattle are tame and domestic while ours are wild and demand not only a larger space for range, but art to hunt and kill them." The comic binocularity here—one profile straight-faced in the "facts," the other in the "art" of ironic hunting—wins the argument, at least on paper, for Corn Tassel. It would appear that Deloria comes by his irony historically.

Homo ludens, Huizinga argues, is *homo* at his best—and *she's* even better humored, reply feminist Indians like Paula Gunn Allen (*The Sacred Hoop*) and Rayna Green (*That's What She Said*) with an Indian twist. Louise Erdrich's richly humorous fictions, next to those of James Welch and N. Scott Momaday, set these feminist arts into ludic play beside the men (are there "humorous" gender differences to be respected among Indians?). Must Indian women "steal" back the languages from the patriarchs, in the way mainstream feminists such as Adrienne Rich break into modern American poetry (Alicia Ostriker, *Stealing the Language*)? If Euroamerican women have fought for a century to be enfranchised, were tribal women ever disenfranchised in their cultures, where the great majority of Indian peoples were matrilocal (perhaps ninety percent, the UCLA sociologist Duane Champagne estimates with me in personal conversation). Rather than "stealing" back the language, literary Indian women may simply be claiming and voicing their native birthrights.

Deloria stings most sharply those he most hopes for—anthros, churchmen, Congress, curious readers. *Custer* and Company sets up cultural-comic confrontations in print: potshots that hit their marks and make us think, even in reaction or disagreement. For a change in Indian–White relations, this constitutes a dialogue, even if printed as an Indian monologue or satiric diatribe. As Deloria writes later with due irony on treaty violations, *We Talk, You Listen.*

Such jibes spark serious play, a form of public teasing to raise important Indian–White issues. Teasing is key to Indian bonding and checking the tribal norms, Deloria notes. The word "teasing," as we know it, comes from the Anglo-Saxon *taesan*, to "pull" or "pluck." It once meant to raise a nap on cloth, now to annoy and entertain by focusing play aggressively toward someone. So tribal teasing, pan-Indian style where Red English is the lingo, targets issues with an attention that roughs its audience affectionately. To tease, to tickle, to tweak—these human acts of humor grant affection masked as aggression. One may tease oneself, but as with most things human, an "other" makes it more fun; three draws a crowd. Jokes work best, Freud thinks, when some*one* has an*other* to amuse a third party.

So when Deloria quips with Algonkians muttering, "There goes the neighborhood!" on the arrival of the pilgrims; or Custer shouting, "Take no prisoners!" at the Little Big Horn; or Red Power AIMsters chanting, "We Shall Overrun" in the 1970s; or warning Black Panthers against playing "Cowboys and Blacks" (more genocide, more reservations?)—this Red satirist is inviting "the others" to joust, yes, but to interact and be part of Native America. Historically, "Whites" invaded "Reds" with enslaved "Blacks," not to mention indentured "Browns" and "Yellows." The native castles—roundhouses, wickiups, teepees, igloos, hogans—were sacked, good "goods" stolen, some ninety-seven percent of the population exterminated, the remaining few "reserved" (for later use?). "Indian giver" is probably the worst joke in our popular lexicon, perhaps a term of racist guilt that inverts true history. An entire hemisphere was taken, not to be given back, and Indians protest. Supplies were always short at the Wounded Knee 1973 military occupation, Carter Camp the Osage warrior recalls: ammunition, cigarettes, and especially toilet paper were precious. So *thank God* for those six little missionary churches in the hamlet, with all the stacks of shiny new Bibles printed on rice paper!

With Custer (who got what glory he was after) there is an absurdist, reverse release for Indian bitterness. It taps the pain of historical statistics, body counts, present poverty and continued suffering. Warriors grow "too old to muss the custard anymore": Deloria plays with folk verbiage, as well as Custer's folly. The triple pun, Custer/mustard/custard, reduces our "hero" to flatulent flan ("too old to cut the mustard" is an old country crack about "breaking wind" in the Midwest). Syllabic nonsense frees us from too much sense, distances us comically from wounded honor, scalp-taking, our losses, their betrayals, and personal fears today of aging and dying, Indian and otherwise. Like the redness of blood, or the jokes about failure, dying is a universal for all human beings (the last joke?). So Indian–White tragedies, through Red humor in context today, transform seriously playful texts: they tell us much about ourselves, American and Native American.

"Friend and Brother!" the Iroquois Red Jacket greets Mr. Cram of the Boston Missionary Society in 1828: the sun is bright, our eyes and ears are open and unstopped, so listen. "Brother! You say there is but one way to worship and serve the Great Spirit. If there is but one religion, why do you white people differ so much about it? Why do not all agree, as you can all read the book?" (*Native American Testimony*, 70). The Iroquois, too, have faiths, Red Jacket assures the missionary, but "We never quarrel about religion. . . ." The slippage here—the split planes of reference, overtly innocent, covertly ironic—involves the kind of grainy humor Huck Finn senses when Colonel

Sherburn faces down the lynch mob. It's like eating bread "that's got sand in it." Back in Boston, Reverend Cram declined to shake Red Jacket's hand, since "there could be no fellowship between the religion of God and the works of the devil." Peter Nabokov recounts: "The Iroquois are said to have smiled" (69).

By 1866 the Chiricahua Apache leader Cochise addressed General Gordon Granger with scathing sarcasm at a truce talk about surrendering to the Tularosa Reservation. "The white people have looked for me long. I am here! What do they want? If I am worth so much why not mark where I set my foot and when I spit?" (*NAT,* 223). It's a challenge of the nature of Old English *flytings*, where the object is to humiliate the enemy satirically. God made the Apaches "not as you," Cochise says, but "born like the animals, in the dry grass, not on beds like you. This is why we do as the animals. . . ." With a mixture of sadness and satire, Cochise reasons: "The Apaches were once a great nation; they are now but few, and because of this they want to die and so carry their lives on their fingernails." The metaphor brilliantly focuses a blade-like irony. "Many have been killed in battle," Cochise goes on. "You must speak straight so that your words may go as sunlight to our hearts. *Tell me, if the Virgin Mary has walked throughout all the land, why has she never entered the wigwam of the Apache?*" (italics as printed, *NAT,* 225). The question seems reasonable enough, though sharply cut. Cochise concludes that he has "no father nor mother; I am alone in the world. No one cares for Cochise." Yet he chooses to stay in his native-born mountains, rather than surrender to White incarceration on a new reservation. "The flies on those mountains eat out the eyes of the horses. The bad spirits live there. I have drunk of these waters and they have cooled me; I do not want to leave here."

Dark Red Humor

Minneconjou Sioux in South Dakota: "For people who are as poor as us," John (Fire) Lame Deer says in the mid-1970s, "who have lost everything, who had to endure so much death and sadness, *laughter is a precious gift*. When we were dying like flies from the white man's diseases, when we were driven into the reservations, when the Government rations did not arrive and we were starving, at such times watching the pranks of a *heyoka* must have been a blessing."

"We Indians like to laugh" (*Lame Deer Seeker of Visions*, 237).

Richard Erdoes came all the way from Freud's Vienna of 1940 to hear Lame Deer in South Dakota thirty years later; the old holy man's recorded words ring true to character. *Heyoka* laughter, the crackling "fire" of his presence, charged his teachings to my students in *The Good Red Road*, along with a pipe blessing and native hospitality. Consider the "precious gift" of Lame Deer's life-story, as told in bricolage through Richard Erdoes during the 1960s and 70s. It corrects, in some comic sense, John Neihardt's tragic narrative of the Oglala Sioux *heyoka* or sacred clown, Nicholas Black Elk from Pine Ridge.

Scholars such as Krupat, Brumble, and Ruppert have taken shots at the Eurocentric misnomer "autobiography" in the "as told to" life-stories of hundreds of Indians (*Recovering the Word*). True enough, silent authors such as Paul Radin or John Neihardt often "spoke for" their informants, since the latter didn't speak or write English. Still, the stories exist as records of intercultural exchange, and DeMallie's work with the Neihardt transcripts, *The Sixth Grandfather*, indicates that little was made up by the intermediary. Neihardt's art was more a matter of mosaic. The critical questions, beyond translation and field accuracy and textual reconstruction, seem ones of dialogical interpretation: What can we make of the text once we have it before us? Can we interpolate the humans behind marks on the page? Rather than play at discrediting texts (the fad these deconstructionist days), what can we do with what we've got? Do we hear any humor in the dry crackle of ethnographic texts?

Lame Deer opens his life-story in a puberty vision pit; to understand the medicine man, he says, we must know the man, so Lame Deer tells of his namesake great-grandfather's death in the 1877 Dakota reserve. General Miles with his grizzly Civil

War recruits came to quell "hostiles." The Bluecoats bolted, and
as he pumped the chief's hand, Miles shouted unsuccessfully,
"*Kola, kola*—friend, friend" (19). Lame Deer comically drops
an ethnic grenade, "It sure was a strange way for friends to drop
in...." Considering the massacre a century ago, this great-
grandson sees his namesake's death from the vision pit, not as
the brunt of Bearcoat Miles's malice, or even through the
soldier's savagery, but ironically: *Tahca Ushte's* rifle hangs on
display at the Heye Foundation in Harlem, the largest holding
(some four million pieces) of Indian artifacts in the world.

A gun is the old way, antiquated, as the museum gathers
White artifacts in Harlem. At best, museum-catching "our"
American Indians seems a callow kind of tourism. Indeed,
March 1986 in upper Manhattan I found such collectibles on
display as Big Foot's pipe tomahawk, Sitting Bull's war club, and
Crazy Horse's medicine society bonnet next to a repeating rifle.
Si-tanka, or Big Foot, the Minneconjou leader dying of pneu-
monia, was labeled "Hunkpapa chief who was massacred, along
with most of his people, at Wounded Knee Creek in 1890."
Down the island that afternoon, I got to the Museum of Natural
History just in time to hear a "Museum Guide" tell her covey in a
strident voice that Plains Indians "died out" because they exterminated the buffalo, on which they solely depended, driving
them over cliffs in "kills," as the diorama showed. She said they
took only what they could carry and left the rest to rot. It was
news to me. "Any reader of Indian novels," the docent went on
to say, "knows that Plains Indians once a year gather, barbecue,
dance around, and pray for a good year" at Sun Dances (hadn't
she told us they "died out" from killing off the buffalo?). Next
door to Indians were exhibits on primates and prehistoric
beasts, an old museum layout.

Lame Deer's dark Red irony is not exactly Western, what
Beckett in *Watt* calls the mirthless, "dianoetic laugh, down the
snout—Haw!—so. It is the laugh of laughs, the *risus purus*, the
laugh laughing at the laugh, the beholding, the saluting of
the highest joke, in a word the laugh that laughs—silence
please—at that which is unhappy" (48). Rather than pathos and
Western *Angst* (Julia Kristeva terms this Western "abjection" in

Powers of Horror), Lame Deer's dark humor biculturally tries to accept what *has* happened in hope that it will not or should not happen again. *Tahca Ushte's* gun gives way to John Fire's hearing aid, whose whistling recalls the spirits' voices in his ears, the healer jokes. This Indian *listens*, learns, and looks for a better way, an Indian–White collaboration with Richard Erdoes, the silent writer, who himself listens and looks as a way to mediate the "differences." These bisociations are rendered and perceived via humor and humanist alternatives to racism and warfare (from John Fire's slouch cowboy hat and seasoned boots, over buckskins and a war bonnet, to Erdoes's own pre-World War II childhood as dark-skinned, Jewish-Catholic-Calvinist "other" to everyone in eastern Europe, a mixed "breed" accepted nowhere until "took in" by Indians in the Dakotas, as he recalls in the Epilogue).

What gives Lame Deer this ability to negotiate atrocity with humor? The *heyoka* tradition certainly trains a native plains wit toward a sacred sense of comic mediation in all things worldly *and* spiritual (the two are one, Lame Deer argues from a Lakota cultural perspective, using an old pot as his homely symbolic stew). And just as the *heyoka* teaches traditional Lakotas the "contrary" or "two-faced" nature of all things (*Iktome* the spider doubles reality, something of a tragicomic figure who mends fissures), so the bonus is a sense of options: nothing is fixed, not even injustice. This single fulcrum divides the tragic sense of end-stopped suffering, a denial of free will or individual ability to change, from comic renewal, a sense of *re*creation, of alternatives, of possibilities. It's an argument between past and future, simplified, a historical determinism transcended by humanist futurity. *Iktome*, the wily spider, is one Lakota agent of comic change, a Trickster weaver and medicine teacher who patches worn webs of history. S(he) births the future and nets flies to feed the young.

Weaving theory into texture, Mary Douglas argues for culture-specific joking contexts the world over. Particularly among African tribes, Douglas sees joking in Radcliffe-Brown's terms, a "permitted disrespect," a subconscious kinship that plays consciously with its own limits. When is an insult not a joke, and vice versa, she asks, and why are some jokes among men not funny in the presence of women? Forming a human Sioux chain to pee down Teddy Roosevelt's nose, as Lame Deer recalls in the 1970s at Mt. Rushmore, may strike a Santee as comic, but probably not a D.A.R. like my mother or a Shriner such as my uncle. "What's the best thing to come out of Nebraska?" a Big Red friend asks me thirty years later in Mazatlin. "I-80," he crows. Jerry Culp now lives in Colorado half the year and runs a golf course the other half in Ogallala, Nebraska. He can joke with me on this issue, since we grew up across the alley in Alliance; but we wouldn't like Californians taking a swipe at our origins. "Why does the wind blow so hard in Wyoming?" he quizzes me on the beach. "Nebraska sucks." It was ten below zero and blowing then on the northern plains; we were sipping sunset margaritas. It seemed funny enough at the time. When Jerry and I were kids together walking to school, this "joke" was a different story.

The point stands: our common past conditions the play connections of joking. Our kinship interconnects comically (perhaps not to "others," but comedy makes them butt, not audience, to our jokes). We laugh at ourselves to "play" with our ties. What struggle we shared we have survived, and we come together to laugh about it, to joke about what-was and where-we-have-come and how-it-all-might-be-fine, even the hurt in the humor. It's a kind of personal tribalism that begins with two people, configurates around families, composes itself in extended kin and clan, and ends up defining a nation. And it's particularly Indian in America.

Comic bonding can pivot on playful baiting, especially between tribes. "What did the Sioux say when he finished his dinner?" my Navajo librarian, Vee Salabiye, asked me one afternoon. She had her own hatchet to bury with the Sioux, and she waited, eyes twinkling. I stood there stoic and she cackled, "Dog gone." Without the infamous "dog-eating" Sioux *heyoka* complex, this joke dies on the vine. Furthermore, it helps to know something about the cultural rivalries between Lakota and Navajo (in many ways they are more alike than most other tribes—the two largest Indian nations, a history of migrations, equestrian hunters, powerful warrior nations, strong matriarchal groups to complement the patriarchies, vision ceremonies, etc.). So, in context, the strange (to "others," not Asians) Sioux custom of eating dog sets the joke; but what triggers our laughter, once the social context is in place? The punch line comes curt, end-stopped, suspended in thought—indeed, "poetic"—a kind of aesthetic (or "economical," Freud would say) microphonemics and mini-grammar. *"Dog gone"* reduplicates the initial phoneme inversely, so we hear a contrary play on the syllable, and its monosyllabic ring—the almost comic vowel swallowed in gutturals—plays back on itself. The sound of English "Siouxed," as it were, rings especially funny to Indian ears. The chug rhyme, *"Dog gone,"* might strike any ear as potentially comic, if not clever in the way children roll words around to explore their full potentials. It's an accessible pun, brilliant in its common economy and clipped linguistic charge.

When one of my Lakota graduate students heard about this Navajo joke, she went to the library and asked, "What's a Sioux picnic?" For a second Vee was silenced. "A six-pack and a puppy," Barbara Feezor chuckled. Without losing a beat, our librarian grinned and shot back, "A beer and a six-pack of puppies?" To twist this dog-gone joke one more time, the Florida State chair of anthropology sent me the following from an Oklahoma Creek (still working on his graduate thesis): "What do the Sioux use for cattle feed?"—"Puppy Chow" (J. Anthony Parades, 17 February 1988).

The pitfalls, perhaps, of such elusive comedy in its Indian contexts abound: whereas Freud glosses all psyches abstractly (the curse of White thinking, Deloria says), Mary Douglas unintentionally imposes an ethnocentric Western bias on *all* social contexts for joking. Both generate systems that break down around Indian humor. Hopefully they help us to see our own margins of error—cultural warp, scientific sophism, academic egoism (more jokes would pique more honest, even more scientific attitudes). Where can their science take us?

culture to Culture

In March 1986 the Center for Great Plains Studies convened an
international gathering of scholars and tribal leaders at the
University of Nebraska. The topic of focus was Indians. The first
Native American graduated from the Lincoln campus only a
decade earlier in 1976, and presently some forty Indians inter-
mixed with the twenty-six thousand Cornhuskers on campus.
For thirteen years Lionel Bordeaux had been president of Sinte
Gleska College, chartered in 1971 by the Rosebud Sioux along
the South Dakota border, Lame Deer's country. He spoke about
one of two four-year accredited and tribally controlled Indian
colleges in America (Navajo Community College is the other).
Sinte Gleska ("Spotted Tail") enrolled some five hundred
students a semester and so far had produced one thousand
G.E.D. graduates where the average reservation education was
less than ten years. "From a cup of coffee to a diploma," Odel
Good Shield said, "that's a long road."

Once there was a late-migrating winter bird, Mr. Bordeaux
began, that procrastinated and finally flew all alone and fell
exhausted into a Nebraska barnyard, only to be crapped on by
a cow. It was revived under the warm cowshit, so the bird
woke up singing. It thought spring had returned early to
Nebraska. A cat heard the chirping, dug the lone bird out of the
dung, and ate it. The moral is succinct: everyone who dumps on
you is not your enemy; everyone who digs you out of the dung is
not your friend; when happy in a warm pile of shit, keep your
mouth shut. To abbreviate pan-tribally—bless the cowshit, fool
the cat, and stay quiet until you know what you're crowing
about.

Now this, to my mind, is a "real" Indian joke, bio- and geo-
specific to the northern Plains. It seems culture-specific to the
Sioux and comically "ludotopic" to Indians today, where time
takes on the flesh of ludic space (improvising from Bakhtin's lexicon in *The Dialogic Imagination* and Huizinga's *Homo
Ludens*). When to move, where to migrate: these issues pre-
occupied Plains tribes for good reasons. The Lakota, by choice

or circumstance, had been semi-nomadic for over a millennium; they relocated up the eastern seaboard, across the Great Lakes when encroached on from the East, and out onto the Plains by the late seventeenth century. There they traveled north and south seasonally with the buffalo herds. The Sioux, as French trappers renamed them "snake" people via the Ojibwa slur, went as far south as Kansas and north to Canada; they were a formidable presence from the Missouri River to Montana. When the horse or "holy dog" (*sunka wakan*) showed up on the Plains magically at the end of the eighteenth century, the Sioux along with the southern Plains Kiowa rode for a century as Plains centaurs, Scott Momaday imagines. In any respect, they moved around, wintered in the Black Hills, saw themselves as brothers to the buffalo, kinsmen of the eagle, and psychic companions with the horse. Spider or *Iktome* tricked the Lakota, two-faced them, teased them, all to help them quick-wittedly survive reality's doublings and illusions. Coyote showed them how to survive on next to nothing. So animals taught, directed and guided Sioux tribes, fed them, carried them across the endless shortgrass prairies, and took them into their natural world in which Indians felt "animal-person."

Bordeaux's little brown bird is a kinsman then, a tribal totem, the world meaning from the Ojibwa "my fellow clansman." The bird's misfortune prefigures our fortune, future, and heuristic comic feast, as in the Christian conception of the "fortunate fall" or *felix culpa*. This nondescript, late-to-learn, misguided little migrator, a sorry pilgrim and generic fool, falls into our laps as a lesson. It obviously has to do with survival, where the weather changes about as quickly as men's minds and the environment remains as relentless as animal hunger. The comic pay-off comes through what we, a "native" audience, hear and learn in The Fall—what we can laugh about by way of learning things useful and perhaps pleasing.

The reversals in the story are characteristic of countless animal stories in the bestiaries of Native America, which Ovid would itch to write down. The weather changes, animals move, some delay. One young naif tarries too long; it falls into the dark soup; the "gods" defecate on it. The innocent wakes up, opens its mouth at the wrong time, and another hungry wayfarer, somewhat cleverer and luckier, satisfies the claws of hunger in late winter. The complexity of the plot, along with its narrative simplicity and down-to-earth basics, flows richly with reversals, surprises, and grim yet funny conclusions. Late fall becomes winter, the bird learns too late, and out of exhaustion and desire fantasizes false spring. A lyric birdsong out of season brings disaster—it's still winter (poor timing), and a hungry cat gets fed. We lose our bird and gain a moral: don't go it alone or attend to the changes, if you must. Know what's going on, but don't think you know it all. Tribe transcends the terminal *first* person, the existential "hero" as clown in communal terms at best. The comic mistake is a valuable teaching. Every Trickster tale in North America turns on this point. There's always hurt in humor, and vice versa, because that's the way things are. It's the way one learns about truth, the hope for survival, and the joy of having survived to the moment. So keep your mouth shut and pay attention. Hence, that infamously clipped Plains plain style, verging on absolute reticence ("yep," "nope," at best "mebbe"), and the mask of the silent warrior, the cigar-store Sioux laughing up his buckskin all the way to the meat cache that gets him through a hard winter.

Surely there's some aggression here, or stricture, what Johan Huizinga calls the *agon* of all play: things hang critically at stake, and talk runs secondary to experience. Just as surely humor comes into play, peppering the pain, even transcending it, for Bordeaux's bird is just word-play, an artistic tale elegantly and still modestly structured, concise, witty. We are *not* little birds. We need not perish in the cowshit. We need only know that we can mistake circumstances, must evade predators, should identify our friends, and want to know the right time to open our mouths. Our lives depend on it.

Lionel Bordeaux *told* this story. It was an "oral" text, a contemporary performance before an audience, tribal in origin, Indian as pumpkins, buffalo and beans. He spoke as one of "the people," unpretentiously streetsmart, scatologically basic, critically sharp to things-as-they-are. As I listened, it seemed that Bordeaux was speaking to me, an alleged specialist in American

Indian Studies. Both of us no doubt felt ourselves as the bird at stake; both of us wanted to survive educational winters, academic cats, departmental barnyard politics. Secretly we were hoping to elude or snatch the cat (if they had wings, the Chinese say, there would be no birds). We were there to talk across the Red-and-White fence, and he told me something interesting: listen, think about it, apply it, and appreciate the art of survival, a critical skill.

Postscript: don't forget the joke. It was a lesson in coding and decoding texts. Rather than the fashion of jamming the reception and littering the texts, one might argue here the ludic reconstruction of a kinetic message and moral. Quicken your wit, temper your ego, work with a contrary world-as-it-is, and hope for better.

Bibliography

Allen, Paula Gunn. *The Sacred Hoop: Recovering the Feminine in American Indian Traditions*. Boston: Beacon Press, 1986.

Bakhtin, Mikhail. *The Dialogic Imagination*. Edited by Michael Holquist. Translated by Michael Holquist and Caryl Emerson. Austin: University of Texas Press, 1981.

Beckett, Samuel. *Watt*. New York: Grove Press, 1959 (1953).

Deloria, Jr., Vine. *Custer Died for Your Sins: An Indian Manifesto*. New York: Macmillan, 1969.

_____. *God Is Red*. New York: Grosset and Dunlop, 1973.

_____. *We Talk, You Listen: New Tribes, New Turf*. New York: Delta Publishing, 1970.

DeMallie, Raymond, ed. *The Sixth Grandfather: Black Elk's Teachings Given to John G. Neihardt*. Lincoln and London: University of Nebraska Press, 1984.

Douglas, Mary. "The Social Control of Cognition: Some Factors in Joke Perception." *Man* 3 (1968): 361–76.

Erdrich, Louise. *Love Medicine*. New York: Holt, Rinehart and Winston, 1984.

Freud, Sigmund. *Jokes and Their Relationship to the Unconscious*. Translated and edited by James Strachey. New York: W. W. Norton, 1960 (1905).

Frye, Northrop. *Anatomy of Criticism*. Princeton: Princeton University Press, 1957.

Green, Rayna, ed. *That's What She Said: Contemporary Poetry and Fiction by Native American Women*. Bloomington: Indiana University Press, 1984.

Huizinga, Johan. *Homo Ludens: A Study of the Play-Element in Culture*. Boston: Beacon Press, 1955 (1944).

Kristeva, Julia. *Powers of Horror*. Translated by Leon S. Roudiez. New York: Columbia University Press, 1982 (1980).

Lame Deer (Fire), John, and Richard Erdoes. *Lame Deer Seeker of Visions*. New York: Simon and Schuster, 1972.

Lévi-Strauss, Claude. *The Savage Mind*. Chicago: University of Chicago Press, 1966 (1962).

Lincoln, Kenneth, with Al Logan Slagle. *The Good Red Road: Passages into Native America*. San Francisco: Harper & Row, 1987.

Momaday, N. Scott. *House Made of Dawn*. New York: Harper & Row, 1968.

Nabokov, Peter, ed. *Native American Testimony. An Anthology of Indian and White Relations: First Encounter to Dispossession*. New York: Harper & Row, 1978.

Neihardt, John G., trans. *Black Elk Speaks: Being the Life Story of a Holy Man of the Oglala Sioux*. New York: Pocket Books, 1972 (1932).

Ostriker, Alicia Suskin. *Stealing the Language: The Emergence of Women's Poetry in America*. Boston: Beacon Press, 1986.

Rourke, Constance. *American Humor: A Study of the National Character*. Garden City: Doubleday, 1953 (1931).

Swann, Brian, and Arnold Krupat, eds. *Recovering the Word: Essays on Native American Literature*. Berkeley: University of California Press, 1987.

Welch, James. *Winter in the Blood*. New York: Harper & Row, 1974.

SINGING THE LAND
Australia in Search of Its Soul

PETER BISHOP

Where nature is prosaic,
Unpicturesque, unmusical and where
Nature reflecting Art is not yet born:—
A land without antiquities....
Barron Field, First Fruits of
Australian Poetry, 1819

According to Jung, "Almost every great country has its collective attitude.... Sometimes you can catch it in a formula, sometimes it is more elusive, yet nonetheless it is indescribably present as a sort of atmosphere that pervades everything...."[1] Jung suggested that the more well-defined a culture, with a solid historical background, the easier it generally was to express its genius in a single phrase. Paradoxically, a relatively young country—such as the United States that Jung visited in the 1920s and which he referred to as childlike, impetuous and naive—could well have "the most complicated psychology of all...." The apparent "simplicity and straightforwardness" of people in such cultures hides a complex fragmentation, a lack both of coherence and of connectedness with the land itself, the ancestral soil.

From the European point of view, white Australia is the youngest of all Western cultures, and one could therefore expect

its psychology to be as complex as its persona is straightfor-
ward. In fact, behind the image it wishes to present to the world
and to itself—confident, egalitarian, anti-authoritarian, outgoing
and so on—lies a far richer, albeit more disturbing,
psychological underworld.[2] Australian cultural identity is
characterized by a troubled sense of place. The search for an
Australian identity, almost a national obsession, has been a pro-
cession of attempts to locate itself in relation to both the land
upon which it rests and also to the geographical-cultural position it occupies on the globe. It is a culture born of desperate exile. Ironically, whilst being the "youngest" culture, it coexists
side by side with the "oldest," that of the Aboriginals whose
tradition is claimed to go back unbroken for over forty thousand
years.[3] At the same time, it is a fragmented culture, where over
forty percent of its present inhabitants were born either overseas
or to parents who themselves came from another country.

1988 witnessed the bicentenary of white settlement and
brought the question of Australian identity into the foreground.
But on the back of this quest have come some grim shadows that
for many years were confined to the outer fringes of white
Australian consciousness. While most whites celebrated, most
blacks mourned two hundred years of conquest, exploitation
and degradation. Such mourning has not escaped the attention
of whites, and many genuine attempts have been made in recent
years to somehow appease not only Aboriginal grief and outrage
but also white conscience, its grief and shame.[4] One of the most
significant, and controversial, gestures reflecting this change of
heart was the handing back to its traditional Aboriginal owners,
in 1985, of Ayers Rock, Uluru, perhaps *the* contemporary symbol of a unified Australian identity.

In addition to a troubled sense of place and a deep, although
often unacknowledged, shame toward the indigenous population is a chronic sense of inferiority. This inferiority complex
has been termed the "cultural cringe," a feeling that perhaps
Australia hasn't really got what it takes to make it in the wider
world.[5] Naturally such a hidden wound produces its own
counterphobic reactions: gruff confidence, brash assertiveness,
a dislike of both those who succeed (the "Tall Poppies") and

those who criticize (the "Knockers"). Some have suggested that this complex stemmed from the appalling convict origins, from Australia's subservient position as a remote colony of the British Empire, designed to produce cheap food and raw materials—a fragile outpost of European civilization surrounded either by the threatening multitudes of Asia or the devouring openness of the Antarctic and Southern Pacific.[6] In the days before modern communications the distances that separated Australians from their kin overseas were awesome, matched only by the vast spaces between settlements on the continent itself.[7] The sense of inferiority has also been attributed to the lack of any war of independence or even a "real" war of conquest.[8] Ironically it was a defeat, at Gallipoli in the First World War, which gave Australians a true sense of national coherence, pride and international confidence.[9]

The Australian inferiority complex stems directly from the problematical relationship between the white culture and the land. Australian literature is replete with references to this relationship. For example, Patrick White has constantly sketched out the wounded, destructive shadow of Australian identity upon the backcloth of its geographical superficiality. In his first novel *Happy Valley* (1939), he showed Australian society and nature to be at odds: "The country existed in spite of the town. It was not aware of it. There was no connecting link."[10] White compared European society with "an ugly scab on the body of the earth. . . ." Time and again the figure of the Aboriginal stands between the transplanted European culture and the alien land, a constant question mark, an enigma, a reminder of guilt, a figure of otherness and yet also of possible connection.

But this sense of inferiority, like that of shame, is a psychological asset. Rather than signifying problems of an "adolescent" culture that need to be grown out of, it keeps the vigorous and buoyant Puer enthusiasm of Australian consciousness in touch with the dark imaginal earth upon which it seeks to base itself and draw nourishment. Inferiority, guilt and shame ground the Australian psyche, give it depth, and aid its search for roots. "Soul is made out of its own defenses."[11] Therapy becomes a process of attuning to the fiction.

Alfred Adler insisted that the inferior places in one's psyche
are, by virtue of the degree of introspection given them, those
with the most potential for soul. Indeed, as James Hillman puts
it, "to feel a sense of soul at all is to feel inferior."[12] An ecological
guilt and shame toward the "Earth" and toward those Earth-
related cultures that have been degraded in the quest to tame
and conquer nature are not confined to white Australia, but can
be seen in Westernized cultures around the globe, particularly
those of Anglo-Celtic origins. Being the youngest such culture as
well as being in direct contact with both the oldest culture and
one of the most ancient lands gives white Australians the
awkward privilege of experiencing this general dilemma in a
painfully raw and relatively unprotected way.[13]

Australia and Elsewhere

Both the Aboriginal culture and the global position of the
Australian continent have a well-established place, albeit a small
one, within the mythic terrain of depth psychology. Australian
Aboriginals come an easy second to black Africans as primary
signifiers of "primitivity" and "Earth-relatedness" in Jung's
opus.[14] Australia also has functioned as a geographical image of
otherness and remoteness. Von Franz, for example, reports that
Jung had letters from "all sorts of places, Australia and elsewhere."[15] Those geographical fantasies of course have a long
history, stretching back to the earliest sixteenth- and seventeenth-century imaginings about a mysterious Southern continent: Terra Australis, Down-Under, an upside-down place
peopled by strange creatures and weird plants, a utopia, a
necessary Southern continent balancing the preponderance of
land massed in the Northern Hemisphere.[16] The first explorers
and settlers encountered a place whose fauna and flora were
totally unfamiliar, which seemed to mock the classification
systems established by Linnaeus, and whose original inhabitants
were like survivors from the most remote reaches of humanity's
past. These images were incorporated right from the start into

Australia's own sense of identity. They are part of its young memory, a memory of its origins.

However, the concerns which have evoked the most powerful stories over the years, which have sustained the deepest hopes, fears and questions, have to do with the land itself. Unlike the United States, Canada, or South Africa, or any of the countries colonized by the Spanish, Portuguese, or French, Australia was settled by Europeans *after* the onset of the industrial revolution. A considerable proportion of its original settler-convicts were landless exiles who had already been brutalized by the formation of an urban industrial workforce.[17] White Australian society therefore inherited a soulless world perspective, forged in Europe, with which to establish itself in an alien land. The Aboriginal culture—with its deep rapport with the land, the profundity of its "Dreaming"—throws the loss of an Anima Mundi perspective in white culture into a sharp and cruel relief. Even Jung used Aboriginal beliefs to highlight the dangers inherent in any new settlement: "Certain Australian primitives assert that one cannot conquer foreign soil, because in it there dwell strange ancestor-spirits who reincarnate themselves in the new-born."[18] When the settlers first arrived, they declared the land "Terra Nullius," unoccupied, empty of previous owners. While such a cruel fiction immediately dispossessed the Aboriginals and precluded any necessity for treaties, it also denied the land its ancestral spirits, emptying it of its previous mythological ground. The land then seemed to confront white settlers as a kind of imaginal tabula rasa. True, it granted a certain freedom to inscribe their own stories unfettered by previous associations, but at the same time it deprived the land of its imaginal nourishment. Patrick White contemptuously refers to "the Great Australian Emptiness," as if the culture itself seems unwilling to delve too deeply into the land for fear of what it might discover.[19] The issue of belatedly making a treaty, acknowledging the primacy of Aboriginal occupation, is a crucial but contentious one in bicentennial Australia.

Jung took the relationship with the Earth very seriously: "The mystery of earth is no joke and no paradox"; "The soil of every country holds some such mystery."[20] For Jung, the "earth" was profoundly connected to "history": "Alienation from the unconscious and from its historical conditions spells rootlessness. That is the danger that lies in wait for the conqueror of foreign lands, and for every individual who ... loses touch with the dark, maternal, earthy ground of his being."[21] In matters relating to the earth, Jung adopted a perspective akin to the Aboriginals for whom the two hundred years of white settlement are but the blinking of an eye. Indeed, Jung even considered his own Swiss roots to be somewhat shallow, going back a mere five hundred years on his mother's side.[22] For Jung, the settlement of Australia would have to be located within a much vaster cultural context: "Our migrations have not yet come to an end. It was only a short while ago that the Anglo-Saxons immigrated from northern Germany to their new homeland ... and it is much the same with practically every nation in Europe."[23] Clearly matters of the Earth are slow and deeply ancient. Australia provides the greatest possible contrast between the ancient and the new, between shallowness and depth, between change and stability, haste and a timeless repose.

In his essay "Mind and Earth" Jung addressed the cultural psyche of comparatively recent settlers in countries such as the United States and Australia. He believed these newcomers to lack a deep ancestral connection with the land in which they now lived. Without this essential grounding there was an excessive split between a high level of consciousness and an unconscious primitivity. This was often experienced as a freedom from old ways, but the result was a large, unacknowledged shadow that came to be projected on the original, earth-oriented inhabitants.[24] Of his experiences in the United States Jung wrote: "You feel free ... yet the collective movement grips you faster than any old gnarled roots in European soil would have done."[25] Time and again in Australian literature, as characters celebrate an apparent freedom from the restraints of the Old World they seem to become more bogged down, their imaginations more circumscribed, either their actions more desperate or their inertia more resigned.[26]

Our Western myths—the root metaphors of our culture, of

our ancestors—have no immediate geographical resonance in Australia. They are out of rhythm with the seasons, with the anti-clockwise rotations of sun and moon. The constellations are inverted. But these myths cannot simply be jettisoned, discarded, nor on the other hand can it be ignored that they are out of place. That is the dilemma. No wonder the Athenians claimed their ancestors were not settlers, but grew from the very soil of the land, from sown dragons' teeth. However, while two hundred years might seem a trivial duration from the perspective of Senex or Great Mother, it is not negligible in terms of, say, Hermes or the Puer. White Australian society has had to bear the scorn of its newness from both the Old World of Europe and from the tradition-bound Aboriginals. From such a literal perspective, it seems doomed to thousands of years of shallowness and psychological inferiority. Clearly, we have entered the well-known debate that circulates around Puer, Senex and Great Mother.

The problem is one of psychological depth, not literal duration. White Australians may well only look back to two hundred years in that land, but their ancestral history is as ancient as anyone else's. It "trails behind it the roots of a thousand ancestral trees."[27] For generations, Australian historical inferiority stood between the present and an archaic past, albeit grounded in other lands. The last twenty years have seen this gap bridged, not only by a focus and value placed on Australia's own history, but on the uniqueness of an Australian view of history, of the past, from "downunder" and "outback." No longer bound to a British parent, an increasingly multicultural Australia is retelling its past from a hundred different sources and traditions—its imaginal roots leading back to Vietnam, Greece, Italy and Yugoslavia as much as to Britain. By what criteria or fantasy does one assess one's cultural identity: duration of presence (Senex / Great Mother), birthright (Great Mother), legal acceptance (Senex), conquest (Hero), and so on? Soul, earth, and history intertwine. The so-called adolescent, or Puer, consciousness of white Australia, with its vulnerability, is not something to be literally grown out of but to be psychologically grown into.

Facing the "Dead" Center, the "Empty" Heart

In a land virtually stripped bare of mythological resonance by the fiction of "Terra Nullius," the immense arid heart—the "outback"—has provided White Australians with both a sense of uniqueness and their greatest enigma. Once the early fantasies of an inland ocean or snowcapped mountains and lush grasslands vanished in the mirage of endless dry horizons, they were left with a country that repeatedly defied pre-existing, nineteenth-century European conceptions of landscape beauty. Until quite recently, the Australian deserts even seemed to elude the inspired comments evoked by other, more glamorous, wilderness regions such as the Sahara or the Arctic. Yet facing the so-called empty heart is a leitmotif of Australia's search for identity, and three recent books succinctly encapsulate the contemporary dimensions of this task.

In his 1982 novel *The Plains* Gerald Murnane tells of a young man, a filmmaker, who arrives in a country town somewhere on "the plains." This is a place that is both inside and yet also outside of Australia. It is both visible and invisible, both physical and metaphorical.[28] The "plains" lie at the very center of the continent, encircled by "outer" Australia—the sterile margins and superficial outer layers. This is a recurrent motif in Australian literature. We can see it not literally, but as a yearning for depth and interiority, to get beyond the mundaneness symbolized by urban Australia.

The vast plains of the center have played a major part in the creation of an Australian identity despite, or perhaps because of, its being one of the most urbanized of countries. The slow pace of most Australian landscapes, their seeming indifference to humanity, the abundance of space continually evoke fears of being devoured, of falling asleep, of passivity. The counterphobic reaction has been predictable: aggression, haste, busyness. As if in direct response to fears of a devouring Great Mother, Australian men have an unenviable reputation with the feminine and women, one in which sexual uncertainty goes hand in hand with aggression and disdain.[29] To go bush has never carried the same individualistic optimism as the equivalent American phrase "to go West." It expresses a collective resistance to urban life, to European cultural values; it celebrates the male bonding of "mateship" and a melancholic eccentricity.

The filmmaker is surely one of the heroes in modern Australia's coming of age, in its fantasy of forging a new, confident identity. In the 1980s the filmmaker has superseded the explorer, pioneer and soldier at the leading edge of Australian self-esteem. In Murnane's book, the filmmaker wants to find the secret essence of the "plains," those immense, seemingly empty flat lands that lie not only at the heart of the continent, but also at the heart of an Australian identity. Coming to terms with this enormous arid center has challenged whites since settlement, alternately fascinating and repelling them, a metaphor of hope and renewal as well as one of tedium and futility. In one Australian film after another, the landscape is a crucial character—an empty space devoid of inhabitants, a signifier of emptiness, yet at the same time a soulful and spiritual focus.[30]

In the novel, exploration begins to reveal subtle variations of detail—light, color, sounds, an abundance of retiring wildlife. We encounter debate about the essence of the plains: does it lie in the scant layer of haze where land and sky meet and merge in the furthest distance or in the very detailed focus on a small, intimate patch immediately underfoot? Murnane calls the people who live on the plains the "inner" Australians.[31] The filmmaker searches for a guide into this region, someone to initiate him into the secrets of the plains so that he too can belong, become an insider. Murnane's filmmaker disappears into the distance, endlessly pursuing a mirage. The plains are "always in the outer darkness. . . . Always the hidden orchestrator of our senses."[32]

Taking up similar themes, *Tracks* by Robyn Davidson tells the true story of the author's journey with three camels and a dog across the center of Australia in the late 1970s. The author and traveler was a young, well-educated, middle-class white woman. For her, Alice Springs symbolized mainstream white culture: soulless, rootless, racist, affluent. Her journey, as recorded in this book, is the story of her attempt to break through to a deeper sense, not just of her own worth, but also of the land.

Like Murnane, Davidson separates Australians into the "outsiders," those living on the coastal regions, and the "insiders" who inhabit the outback. In both cases, outsiders equals superficiality, unrelatedness. This equation occurs time and again throughout Australian literature, as the shadow of the Australian Puer psychology is projected on the urban centers, while the "dead" or "red" center assumes the status of unequivocal purity and psychological meaningfulness. In the late nineteenth century the city was imagined as a danger to "racial and national health," whereas now it is more likely considered a threat to individual well-being.[33] Davidson writes: "To enter that country is to be amazed by space and humbled by the most ancient bony, awesome landscape on the face of the earth. It is to discover the continent's mythological crucible, the great outback, the never-never, that decrepit desert land of infinite blue air and limitless power."[34]

The original inhabitants of this region naturally take on some of its numinosity, and the unwanted shadow is unceremoniously dumped on her own, rejected culture: "whinging convicts," she calls her ancestors; "the shit of humans is harder to take than that of camels."[35] But much to her dismay she can't seem to break into this mythic center. Of course she *physically* reaches her goal, the geographical "center," but is unable to "be there," to fully experience the place as she so much desires. Around and around in circles she goes, both physically and in her mind, looking for a way in. "I was aware only of a flatteningness, a lack of substance in everything. My steps felt achingly slow, small and leaden. They led me nowhere. Step after step after step, the interminable walking dragged out, pulling my thoughts downward into spirals. The country seemed alien, faded, muted, the silence hostile, overwhelming."[36] She is like a devotee of Artemis, desperate about her inability to find the sacred solitude and untouched wilderness of the Goddess.

Significantly, it is an Aboriginal male elder who becomes her guide, her psychopomp. Through him she comes at last to that "inner" place. The elder becomes an exemplary figure: "healthy, integrated, whole . . . he had strength, warmth, self-possession, wit, and a kind of rootedness, a substantiality that immediately commanded respect.''[37] Gone was her alienation: "the country had changed dramatically. . . . Bright green peeked out of the valleys and chasms. . . . The sense of space, clean bright limitless space was with me again. . . . Time melted—became meaningless. . . . I was a different person. . . . I . . . had entered a different world—a parallel universe.''[38]

David Malouf's *An Imaginary Life* seems at first to have little to do with Australia.[39] It tells the story of the poet Ovid's exile from Rome, his gradual reconciliation to his fate and then his subsequent journey deeper into exile toward his spiritual and psychological emancipation. Ovid is banished to live at the very fringe of the Empire, among primitive tribes who neither speak Roman nor tend gardens. They have no literature. Beyond these crude villages lies the unpopulated vastness of the open steppes, the unbounded plains where even more uncivilized tribes roam and from where they periodically emerge to terrorize those who inhabit the frontier. The Australian resonance is clear, as is the psychological metaphor: rejected by the Senex, the ego finds itself at the very edge of the known, civilized world. Utterly out of place, it stands almost defenseless on the edge of the immense unknown. The sophistication of life in Rome, at the center of the Empire, is not only useless in such circumstances, it is a hindrance, a burden, a source of anguished longing for what one can never return to. Ovid cries, ''my soul aches for the refinements of our Latin tongue.''

But his initial sense of desolation is replaced by a gradual resignation as he finally accepts he can never go home. Paralleling an Australian coming of age, he then begins to explore his place of exile and to formulate a new set of references. He goes for long walks, learns the language and local names for things, begins to value the difference between the raw vitality of this culture and the Roman. Like Murnane and Davidson, Malouf (through Ovid) denigrates the soft life in urban centers and praises the veracity of a more basic, unrefined life closer to the land. Initially he sifts through his attachment to his original home, his resentments against family and society.

He then catches a glimpse of a wild boy, a figure with whom he used to converse as a child but who vanished when he grew up. The rich, relatively unrestrained imagination of childhood, once banished, now returns in old age, though dirty and ugly at first sight. With the help of the villagers the child is captured. Finally, Ovid enters into a long, mutually educative relationship with the child. Eventually they flee together into the depths of the vast plains, Ovid, the old poet in exile, being led by the wild child, a kind of raw Hermes-Mercurius. Finally, Ovid experiences an ecstatic death in the embrace of boundless space and light. Without reducing this story into a programmatic parallel with the historical search for an Australian identity, we can nevertheless detect the essential mythological motifs: exile, Empire, primitive tribes, vast plains; the split between earthy primitiveness and decadent urbanization; the struggle between Puer, Senex and Great Mother eventually resolved, as in so many Australian novels, by an ecstatic, almost cosmic, embrace of death in the arms of the Mother.[40]

These stories present us with three images of the Australian dilemma—exile from the ancestral mythology and its imaginal ground, as well as the struggle to find new roots, to learn how to belong in an alien land. But in each of these stories a reconciliation with the land, with the great space at the heart of an Australian identity, has been achieved only by vilifying and rejecting urban living and mainstream white culture. It is surely too easy to dump the unwanted shadow of one's culture on the outer fringes of the continent and to embrace the imagined untouched purity of both the central desert and its inhabitants.

Exile is the shadow of belonging. They go together. As a root metaphor of Australian culture, exile is not a problem to be eliminated but a fundamental, archetypal reality to be endured and deepened.

Repopulating the Emptiness

Aboriginals must regularly perform "increase" ceremonies at sacred rites—singing, dancing, telling stories of the ancestral creatures—otherwise they believe that the flora and fauna will die. And of course, they will die, perhaps not literally, but imaginally, symbolically, and then who cares what happens. "In Aboriginal belief, an unsung land is a dead land: since if the songs are forgotten, the land itself will die."[41] The central wilderness, the "Terra Nullius," has resisted European attempts to populate it, both physically and mythically, yet white culture has realized that here lies the key to its identity and its sense of inferiority.

When original settlers declared Australian birds songless and the flora dull, associations sprung up to repopulate the land with more familiar species imported from Europe. The result was often an ecological disaster.[42] Mining and tourism have become the new fantasy by which to both populate the outback and to make it profitable. Ayers Rock, a geographical feature climbed by a mere twenty-four people between 1931 and 1946, has become the focus of this repopulating with over 150,000 struggling to its summit in 1988. The bizarre murder case of Azaria Chamberlin and the dingo focused the pathologized fantasies of an entire continent on the "rock."[43] The center is an imaginal lodestone. The question is how to imaginatively populate the "gap," the "emptiness" between "coast" and "center." Rather than searching for large, bold, or heroic responses, we might find it is the small details, the subtle images which call for attention. These can be found in the landscape painters of the early twentieth century, particularly the Heidelberg school, as well as in the poetry and prose of this period as white Australians began to forge a new aesthetic peculiar to their conditions.[44] Such a fledgling aesthetic celebrates solely neither the Great Mother nor the heroic pioneers and explorers, but seeks to recognize a beauty that had previously slipped through the grid of Western aesthetics and had hence been discarded.

This conclusion finds contemporary expression in each of the three stories discussed above. Ovid begins to notice details of vegetation, of sound and smell in the landscape that had previously seemed so desolate. With this attention, this attuning, comes the first flash of color. An imaginal spring awakens in Ovid's soul. Robyn Davidson has to relinquish her abstractions of bold feats, heroic endeavors of preconceived notions of the "center." Then, unexpectedly, she becomes aware of details—

noises, tracks, colors, silences. The filmmaker in *The Plains* also has his large-scale expectations stripped away and begins to involve himself in the ever-shifting plurality of sensual details. The desperate search for the "center" is reinforced by the singleness of the continent itself, both of which have come to symbolize the "one" Australia. But, whether rushing to the "pure" center or clinging to the "soft" outer edge, one can all too easily lose the richness and detail of the ground in-between.

Just over thirty years ago, a foreign power, Britain, was invited to undertake atmospheric testing of nuclear bombs in the desert just a few hundred miles to the north of Adelaide, the capital of South Australia. At the time it seemed eminently sensible to most Australians: after all, *the land was empty.*[45] Now such an event would seem outrageous, because that land, for all its aridity and desolation, is no longer considered meaningless; neither are the rights of fauna and flora, however sparse and unspectacular to the European way of thinking. A generation of bush walkers, conservationists, even tour operators and mining companies have imaginatively populated the desert with meaningful images. Aboriginal place names are finding their way onto maps with increasing frequency as the legacy of "Terra Nullius" is healed. What mythological sense, for example, can we make of the idiosyncratic convergence of anti-uranium mining, Aboriginal land rights, and wilderness protection? This is the most potent symbolic alliance in contemporary Australia and reflects the deep concern about the "land"—its central place in Australian identity, in Australia's global responsibility, in the debt owed to the Aboriginals.

In a recent paper James Hersh refers to the *Orestia* to insight the struggle between *ethnos* (obligations based on kin, blood, people, and earth) and *polis* (social contract, constitution, city, and civic duty).[46] As defenders of *ethnos*, the Furies contemptuously refer to the laws of *polis* as being young, as abstractions without true, ancestral foundations. They insist upon the ancient primacy of *ethnos* and are outraged at the dismissal, or even ignorance, of its claims. Unless they are allowed a respected place in the *polis* they will extract vengeance. Here is the Australian dilemma, as two hundred years of white culture are confronted by forty thousand years of Aboriginal. The fiction of "Terra Nullius" insulted *ethnos* and the Furies. Aboriginals on the whole have angrily rejected the idea of simple assimilation into *polis*. They want recognition and a place for their ancient ways. This is the psychological significance of the call for a treaty. Although on one level it could well be just a meaningless slip of paper, it does begin to recognize the paradox of belonging to both a nation and a race. Even though white Australia cannot simply adopt the myths of the Aboriginals, these stories evoke an appreciation of the land that is neither literal nor just metaphorical. They call to a deepening, an earthy grounding, of the psychological foundations of *polis*, of white civic, democratic culture. Out of the inferiority a new aesthetic is slowly emerging.

1. C. G. Jung, *CW* 10, §§ 972, 946, 980.

2. See, for example, the review of the film *Crocodile Dundee*, by V. Brady: "Evading History," *Australian Society* 7/3 (March 1987): 33–34. Also, a country where one tenth of the population owns sixty percent of the wealth while another tenth of the population lives below the poverty line is scarcely as egalitarian as many would like to believe.

3. See M. Charlesworth, H. Morphy, D. Bell and K. Maddock, eds., *Religion in Aboriginal Australia: An Anthology* (St. Lucia: University of Queensland Press, 1986); and W. Stanner, *White Man Got No Dreaming* (Canberra: Australian National University Press, 1979).

4. See H. Reynolds, *The Other Side of the Frontier* (Townsville: James Cook University Press, 1981); J. Gribble, *Dark Deeds in a Sunny Land* (Perth: University of Western Australia Press, 1988); R. Evans et al., *Race Relations in Colonial Queensland* (St. Lucia: University of Queensland Press, 1988); see also the novel by Xavier Herbert, *Capricornia* (Sydney: Angus and Robertson, 1956) or Judith Wright's *The Generations of Men* (Melbourne: Oxford University Press, 1981) for damning fictional insights into white Australia's degradation both of Aboriginal culture and the land.

5. See J. Carroll, ed., *Intruders in the Bush: The Australian Quest for Identity* (Melbourne: Oxford University Press, 1982). Some believe that this cultural cringe is a result of elitist aspirations and a denial of the "true" Australian culture represented by the pub, the beach, vegemite, barbecues, and so on, e.g., J. Fiske, B. Hodge, G. Turner, *Myths of Oz: Reading Australian Popular Culture* (Sydney: Allen and Unwin, 1988).

6. See some of the essays in Carroll, *Intruders in the Bush*; also A. Moorehead, *The Fatal Impact* (Harmondsworth: Penguin, 1968) locates the "discovery" of Australia within the context of the European encounter with the Antarctic and with the cultures of the South Pacific; also, I. Donaldson, ed.,

Australia and the European Imagination, monograph 1, Humanities Research Centre (Canberra: Australian National University, 1982).

7.   For a controversial discussion on the theme of distance in Australian identity, see G. Blainey, *The Tyranny of Distance* (Melbourne: Sun Books, 1966).

8.   See chapters one, two and four in Carroll, *Intruders in the Bush*. In order to uphold the fantasy of "Terra Nullius," the sustained, widespread, organized, and frequently highly successful Aboriginal resistance to white "invasion" has consistently been ignored. For a revised view see Reynolds, *The Other Side of the Frontier*.

9.   B. Gammage, "Anzac," in Carroll, *Intruders in the Bush*; also, the popular and influential film by Peter Weir, *Gallipoli*.

10.   D. Tacey, *Patrick White: Fiction and the Unconscious* (Melbourne: Oxford University Press, 1988), xvi. This is an important and controversial in-depth study, firmly based in Jungian scholarship.

11.   J. Hillman, *Healing Fiction* (Barrytown, New York: Station Hill Press, 1983), 99.

12.   Ibid.

13.   Since European settlement, 78 plant, 1 bird and 12 species of mammal have become extinct, while 182 plant, 18 bird, 2 reptile and 23 mammal species are now endangered. On the other hand, Australia has been in the forefront of wilderness conservation ever since the opening of one of the world's first national parks in 1879.

14.   E.g., C. G. Jung, *CW* 5, §§ 213, 215, 220, 226, 671; *CW* 9, i, §§ 224, 226n.; *CW* 12, § 171; *CW* 13, §§ 128, 130n.14; *CW* 14, § 162n.218; "The Psychology of the Transference," *CW* 16. See also E. Neumann, *The Origins and History of Consciousness* (Princeton: Princeton University Press, 1978), 288–90.

15.   M-L. von Franz, *Puer Aeternus* (Santa Monica: Sigo Press, 1981), 44; also R. Grinnell, *Alchemy in a Modern Woman* (Dallas: Spring Publications, 1973, rpt. 1989), 79–80, 87–88, 93–94, discusses a dream of Australia by a European woman in which that continent signifies somewhere that is opposite to her world, a kind of absolute geographical otherness.

16.   For example, on Australian "weirdness" see the extraordinary collection of literary references to the "kangaroo" (from D. H. Lawrence, Lautréamont, Alfred Jarry, James Joyce and many others) in the novel by Murray Bail, *Homesickness* (Ringwood, Victoria: Penguin, 1980). This is discussed in detail by N. Jose, "Cultural Identity," in *Australia: The Daedalus Symposium*, ed. S. Graubard (Sydney: Angus and Robertson, 1985). Originally published as a complete issue of the *Journal of the American Academy of Arts and Sciences*, this is a most useful introduction to Australian culture. See Moorehead, *The Fatal Impact*, 150–51, for comments on the utopian impulse of the European discoverers of Australia.

17.   M. B. and C. B. Schedvin, "The Nomadic Tribes of Urban Britain: A Prelude to Botany Bay," in Carroll, *Intruders in the Bush*; also S. Nicholas, ed., *The Convict Workers: Reinterpreting Australia's Past* (Sydney: Cambridge University Press, 1988).

18.   Jung, *CW* 10, §§ 103, 969, 979.

19. Quoted in Jose, "Cultural Identity," 317.

20. Jung, *CW* 10, §§ 18, 19, 68, 968.

21. Ibid., § 103.

22. Ibid., § 909.

23.ʳ Ibid., § 1001.

24. Ibid., § 103.

25. Ibid., §§ 957, 928.

26. For example, this tension between a sense of freedom and one of being held fast can be seen in Patrick White's fiction (Tacey, *Patrick White*, xiii,xvi); or in the characters in Helen Garner's novel *Monkey Grip* (Jose, "Cultural Identity," 329).

27. J. Hillman, "Senex and Puer," in *Puer Papers*, ed. J. Hillman (Dallas: Spring Publications, 1979), 6, discusses history as a psychological reality, inherent within the psyche, and not merely an accumulation of past, external events: "Without the sense of soul, we have no sense of history."

28. G. Murnane, *The Plains* (Ringwood, Victoria: Penguin, 1984).

29. See A. Summers, *Damn Whores and God's Police* (Ringwood, Victoria: Penguin, 1980); also K. Dempsey, "Mateship in Country Towns," in Carroll, *Intruders in the Bush*.

30. See J. Clancy, "Film: The Renaissance of the Seventies," in Carroll, *Intruders in the Bush*; also, R. Gibson, "Camera Natura: Landscape in Australian Feature Films," *Framework* 22/23 (Autumn 1983).

31. Murnane, *The Plains*, 12, 17, 25–29, 36–38, 52–53.

32. Ibid., 38, 68–72, 86, 104.

33. R. Davidson, *Tracks* (London: Granada, 1982); on the early antagonism to the city, see J. Hirst, "The Pioneer Legend," in Carroll, *Intruders in the Bush*, 31.

34. Davidson, *Tracks*, 37.

35. Ibid., 22–23, 30, 33–35.

36. Ibid., 141–42, 150.

37. Ibid., 161.

38. Ibid., 161, 174, 177, 180.

39. D. Malouf, *An Imaginary Life* (Sydney: Picador, 1980); see also his novels *Johnno* (Harmondsworth: Penguin, 1976) and *12 Edmondstone Street* (London: Chatto and Windus, 1988) for a concern with the intimate details, the poetics, of Australian urban space. For a fuller, imaginal reading of *An Imaginary Life*, see my "David Malouf and the Language of Exile," *Australian Literary Studies* 10/4 (1982).

40. E.g., in Patrick White's *The Tree of Man* and *Voss* (see Tacey, *Patrick White*).

41. B. Chatwin, *The Songlines* (London: Picador, 1988), 58; for a detailed anthropological study, see T. Strehlow, "Geography and the Totemic Landscape in Central Australia," in *Australian Aboriginal Anthropology*, ed. R. Berndt (Perth: University of Western Australia Press, 1970), especially 133–35; also, Charlesworth et al., *Religion in Aboriginal Australia*; R. Tonkinson, *The Mardudjara Aboriginals* (New York: Holt, Rinehart and Winston, 1978); M. Eliade's *Australian Religion* (Ithaca: Cornell University Press, 1973), although

dated, remains an excellent introduction; see also D. Bird Rose, "Exploring an Aboriginal Land Ethic," *Meanjin* 47/3 (1988).

42.   A. Frost, "The Conditions of Early Settlement," in Carroll, *Intruders in the Bush*, 18; E. Rolls, *They All Ran Wild* (Sydney: Angus and Robertson, 1969).

43.   A. Hamilton, "Spoon-Feeding the Lizards: Culture and Conflict in Central Australia," *Meanjin* 43/3 (1984); and D. Johnson, "From Fairy to Witch: Imagery and Myth in the Azaria Case," *Australian Journal of Cultural Studies* 2/2 (1984), as well as the 1988 film *Evil Angels.*

44.   E.g., J. Manton, *Australian Painters of the Heidelberg School* (Melbourne: Oxford University Press, 1980); A. McCulloch, *The Golden Age of Australian Painting: Impressionism and the Heidelberg School* (Melbourne: Lansdowne Press, 1969); also, for one of the most successful contemporary landscape painters, see P. McCaughey, *Fred Williams* (Sydney: Bay Books, 1980).

45.   For a discussion of the circumstances among the Aboriginal people most affected by the atomic testing, see M. Brady, "Leaving the Spinifex," *Records of the South Australian Museum* 20 (May 1987): 35–45.

46.   J. Hersh, "From *Ethnos* to *Polis*," *Spring 1985*: 56–73.

VARIATIONS ON THE PLAY BETWEEN GODS AND PEOPLE

JUDITH GLEASON

Program Notes

Is it not possible now to begin to speak of soul and self in two languages: an African, for example, and a European?

African gods in diaspora provide expressive means of self-integration within New World religious communities whose adherents for the most part are not culturally committed to psychological thinking—a hermeneutic dependent upon European notions of the person as self-contained, self-activated, and set off against its natural and social contexts. Although individually aware of personality changes as a result of their development as mediums and healers, the initiated participants of Afro-Caribbean religions don't have the habit of discussing them. They will talk gratefully about the objective difference the god they serve has made in their lives—recovered health, a steady job, a successful pregnancy—or testify to increase of confidence, energy, direction, calm and power; but ordinary conversation (correlative to non-directive field work) is unlikely to verge off into a subjective assessment of that crucial relationship between "head-ruling" spirit and human being which presumably exists as an ongoing inner dialogue, whether or not cultural convention encourages either extended pondering thereupon or articulation of such personal matter to others.

Psychological evolutionism is suspect. No longer is it tenable
to consider the manipulation of liturgical symbols and symbolic
behavior in expressive religions like those derived from traditional African practice as a poor alternative to the solitary
discipline of introspection. Apparent differences in talk about
the gods suggest differing cultural emphases and habits of
thought thereby generated. People who spontaneously reflect
upon themselves and come to view with some critical detachment collective values and lifeways can be found in any culture.
(In traditional anthropological practice these reflective ones present themselves as potential "informants.") Similarly, those who
move their beliefs into the "other's" spiritual territory come bag
and baggage. Black baptisms rolled the Jordan out of its
cramped bed. And nowadays when Afro-Americans convert
back to the ancestral religion, they bring the Preacher with
them.

Watery threads of tributaries of all the world's rivers are
searching out replenishing sources these days. Those of European ethnic origin have turned to Afro-Caribbean religion for
deeper self-definition; if they came with the habit of introspection, they have not lost it. Therefore, in search of empirical
evidence of the inner drama going on between person and god,
I turned for help to three colleagues literate in both languages.

All three women on my mind, those whose generous collaboration in reality produced the reveries to follow, have
Ph.D.s, but in different fields, reflecting their different purposes
in life, fields in turn presupposing modes of inquiry which have
further determined the way they conceive of themselves and
their religious experience. Not only are we sister academics, but
cult colleagues. Somehow each of us has managed a tentative
synthesis between models of the self appropriate to who we are,
the work we do, and the African belief system which enables us
to contain, expressively to transform, and eventually to make
sense of else inexplicable suffering, counter-productive behavior, curious intimations of "otherness."

On such familiar ground investigatory power is overtly shared;
so any distorting dangers of intrusive, directive research techniques can be immediately and humorously processed. In order

to focus our talk I set each of us a common task which, assuming continuity of consciousness between person and coopting god, would *ab initio* dramatize differences. Thus, in what we all recognized to be a playful spirit, everyone was to take the Myers-Briggs (personality) Type Indicator test twice. The first time through I asked them to imagine that their "head-ruling" spirit was answering the questions. The second taking of the test should be by their ordinary selves. Putting the graphed outcomes of the computer-processed tests side by side would produce a group of approximate ego–Self axes at this moment in time. That the Self might be a Yoruba Orisha from a pagan pantheon come mysteriously to roost in a European soul is certainly a post-Jungian phenomenon. And that the gods' responses should be imagined on paper rather than spoken in trance is a bit unorthodox from the African standpoint.

By "African" only a fraction of the continent is here implied, and for historical reasons. The highly articulated polytheistic structures of Yoruba-speaking peoples and their westerly neighbors, who speak Fon, provided the armature for the most important of the New World religions. Therefore, though one of the women interviewed has linked up with a version of the Yoruba religion developed in Cuba, another with Brazilian candomblé, and a third with Haitian vodu, the divinities of their experience are all part of the same archetypal system. Though they have never met each other, they have powerful images of each others' gods.

Indispensable to the progress of our project, all would agree, are the mythological linkages between Oya, the researcher's goddess, and those of her interlocutors, two of whom are dedicated to Oshun, with whom Oya stands in a sisterly, co-wife relation. A third element is added by Ogun, god of iron and war, valiantly carried by the woman whom I have called "Clara."[1] Both Oya and Ogun are considered *lele* ("heavy" or "strong") as opposed to cooler divinities like Oshun. Though myth and ritualized play often show these two engaged in furious combat (Oya, the tornado, wields a lightning sword), long, long ago they cohabited, and Oya's bellows remains an essential furnishing of Ogun's forge.

Though the gods are here, we are not at the source. A major difference between "the religion" as practiced in the New World and how things are done in West Africa is that over here, instead of inherited lineage-group worship of characteristic gods ("family madness"), an entire pantheon or even various "nations" of divinities are collocated under one roof. On the personal level this has resulted in the oracular assignment of a secondary Orisha (who does not possess the person) to initiates of the Yoruba religion in Brazil or Cuba and the possibility of being possessed by a spirit of each "nation" composing the Haitian vodu system.[2]

These secondary spirits added texture to our talk, reflective of the manner in which their in-dwelling counterparts complicate and enrich character. Though personality typology provided us with a useful grid upon which to plot variance—to look at our gods as vectors moving us in and out of the world in various co-efficient modalities—as an artificial construct (albeit indubitably quaternioned) it didn't generate either excitement or new meta-knowledge for us. That map didn't descry further territory. But the archetypal system in which we worked surprisingly seemed as a result of our attentiveness to be lighting up new corners of itself as though intentionally moving toward insights into its own mysterious structure!

As shared words and collaborative time brought me close to their human carriers, so Oshun and Ogun became increasingly intelligible modes of being in the world. A segment of the Yoruba cosmos was being made more visible than previously seen in ceremonies. Old myths took on new resonance. And gradually the mirror turned around as Oshun's and Ogun's carriers were naturally drawn to reflect upon Oya's test results in relation to those of the narrator. Thus to watch the goddess passing through me and through the whole process at a certain benevolent distance was an experience unthinkable before.

Variations

CORINNE—*Something in me was resigned to being an impoverished academic. Yet I used to like to dance, to go to parties; and I have always loved beautiful things.* She is living in upstate New York in a clapboard house which the previous owners left in a state of disrepair. Her husband is away for the day teaching in a neighboring town. Her two-year-old is with the older woman who takes care of the child at her own home when Corinne is doing editorial work. It is a warm fall afternoon. Two chairs have been set outside the kitchen door. We relax in the sun and in each other's company. There is a lot to say. We have exchanged letters, but this is the first time we have met face to face.

Corinne's white head-wrap dramatizes the darkness of her eyes—almond shaped like those of a Byzantine mosaic—and the delicate bone structure of her face. The devotional songs Corinne translated from the Sanscrit as part of her doctoral work have recently been published. It's her first book, a true accomplishment. About the same time that the book came out Corinne emerged from an initiation room somewhere in Brooklyn. Seated upon the traditional throne, dressed as the goddess Oshun, she looked (so her husband reports) like Cleopatra. Now, dressed all in white for the required year, Corinne is taken by the local people to be some sort of nun, perhaps a Sufi. They can't figure out what the outfit means. Gypsy? (All those sacred bracelets.) So you look a bit exotic. You can handle it.

No, Laksmi was not the goddess I was consciously interested in. All that splendor. I had no idea I could ever have a piece of that. At the time, when I was in India, I was interested in the Kali type—wild, independent. That's what's supposed to be sitting right here, opposite. We laugh. But sometimes I feel terribly tamed, I tell her.

Initially free to come and go in the world, able to live on a pittance between scholarships, the graceful young graduate student returns to see her options narrowed to a corridor of departmental offices and finally to a single room with only one exit. This part of Corinne's story is not unique. Sexual politics seem

especially ugly in high-minded Academe, where a professor sta-
tioned to write the crucial recommendation gets up from his
desk and crudely attempts to lock the door. Throwing her intellectual aspirations back in his face, the student flees bodily.
Her disillusion won't scar him. He manages to blackball her in a
dissertation committee meeting. What? Her own advisor? Cause
for some knowing winks exchanged among colleagues. It's a
war of nerves now which eventually she will win, but at what
cost? A young man working in the departmental library notices.
"It seems as though you need protection," the young man says,
offering his friendship. "You could go for a reading. You could
wear beads." Resilience. When social reality fails, one's spon-
taneous recourse is often magical. Subsequently, Corinne's
careful work found allies on her dissertation committee. Under
pressure from them, perhaps fearing ridicule, her assailant was
forced to sign his name to her dissertation.

She hasn't been near the university since. Another press
published her annotated translations. She and the young man
with the beads became engaged, then married. But still, for a
long time afterward, *I felt like a dried-up sponge. Whereas I had
thought that some shift had taken place in my personality, I
think now that Oshun–Laksmi was there in me, with me all
along. These last few years of shrinkage, dryness, poverty-
leanings were imposed by the goddess herself. She took away so
that I would come to Her to get it all back. Working up my
health again, I'll also be working up in a new, or intensified,
way my Oshun-ness: art and refinement, the higher consciousness centers of creativity.*

But messages from Oshun continue to come from deep within
the body. In Yoruba thought, conception and the gestation
process fall within Her province. As soon as the child is born,
another goddess, Yemoja, Mother-of-the-waters, is invoked for
protection. To Oshun belongs the womb, to Yemoja the cra-
dling arms and cradle songs. Corinne's husband, the young man
who noticed and offered protection, is a medium of Yemoja.
When Corinne emerges from her incubation, again he will be
there for her. But she cannot emerge too soon. There had
been some danger, apparently, of premature birth. Not long

before our interview, ill with chills and fever, Corinne in a dream felt Oshun draw close to her. *Wrap yourself completely in the sheet,*[3] *the goddess said. Let it surround you with its shape.* The shape was that of an elongated egg. *Stay in the shell, the goddess was telling me. I have not finished brooding on you, warming you. It is not yet time to hatch.* Some days later Corinne recalled a verse from a Sanscrit hymn which her "rational translator's mind" had been unable to find English words for, words which would not "seem silly and punning." The sense of the verse, suddenly clarified by the dream, was as follows: *O, may I be an egg nourished by intense devotion so that one day I may burst forth, a mighty bird, and soar to the heights of spiritual realization.*

It is difficult for Corinne to imagine the face of her goddess right now or to imagine how she herself will come to be seen by the outside world. They are brooding together in a timeless, mythical matrix. *My personality was in shattered pieces. She is molding me.* Corinne's the devotion, Oshun's the answering grace. Though her initiation was ritually begun in a Spanish-speaking Santero's house in Brooklyn, Corinne's religious sensibility took imaginative shape in Sanscrit.

Meanwhile, practical difficulties continue to dog the little household in their clapboard cottage upstate. Though her husband has a steady job and though Corinne herself has been busy with freelance editorial work, leaks, drafts, clogged pipes, poor wiring, and automotive breakdowns drain financial resources and put an untoward stress on day-to-day living. "Come to terms with me," the practical world continues to insist. But how? *Of all things, real estate has come to seem an attractive possibility,* Corinne writes. Already she has studied for and passed the exams required for licensing. *I love matching up people with nice situations. I love riding around looking at property and homes and how people use their space.*

To have asked Corinne while in a sacred, liminal state to fill out a simplistic questionnaire might seem ridiculous, if not impious, had she not insisted that she enjoyed the opportunity to chart the shifting viewpoints symbolized by "me" and "Oshun." Corinne imagines Oshun's taking a much more con-

servative, even "stuffy," stance than she herself on certain
issues, like planning instead of going with the flow, like commit-
ting Herself to fixing up a stationary home. Corinne has a ten-
dency to wish, even to think, herself invisible. It was a defense
she developed while traveling alone in India. Oshun, needless to
say, insists on being a gracious, unforgettable presence—a
queen of both hearts and diamonds.

These shifts are reflected on the Type Indicator graph as
retrenchments of intuition and feeling toward the mean, as a
shift from perception to judgment, and as a bold swing into ex-
troversion. So Corinne imagines Oshun radiating feeling into a
responsive community. Corinne herself takes a lively interest in
the shifting allegiances between gods and people going on in the
Santería house where she was initiated. Those parts of her letters
recounting transposed heads and their rulers call to mind last
minute elopements between lovers disguised in the Forest of
Arden or under the spell of Puck's midsummer mischief. It's
romantic comedy, a Santería soap opera. Who's who? A supposed votary of Yemoja gets taken by Oshun at the last moment.
This sort of confusion wouldn't occur in a traditional society.
But when the core self is split into mutually unintelligible nu-
clei—an "archipelago" (André Green's phrase)—of selflets, a
god comes along and doesn't know which to alight on.

Thus, as Oshun broods upon Corinne, She at the same time
pulls her imagination out into the world, toward real estate and
toward real people mixing and matching guardian spirits. Here is
Oshun the matchmaker at work, helping people to move into
convenient spaces with congenial partners. Here is Oshun the
seamstress at work fashioning a quilt of society, of psyche. The
cosmic egg elongates. Along a horizontal axis of feeling a healing
tension is set up between inner and outer.

Meanwhile, a vertical drama of integration is going on as
well—a unification of opposites meaty and ethereal. Shortly
after her initiation Corinne dreamed the following:

> Some men are standing around. Greasy mechanics. One is
> stocky, muscular, with a reddish, beefy face, all oily with
> mechanics' grease. He looks right at me and reads what my

mind is thinking. "Beefy." So with a wink of his mischievous eye he extends his hand to me. It is a hand made like a steak. Red meat, succulent fat, T-bone. This revives a delicious memory of when I used to enjoy steak. I keep looking. Eyes still twinkling, he keeps extending the hand to me, thought-saying: "This religion isn't all brawn, all animal sacrifices and meat-eating, all illiterate jibaros. Here, look what I have for you, my daughter." And then I see what he's holding on his palm—a tantric symbol, an intricate design involving Sanscrit letters and depictions of the Goddess. The vision was crystal-clear [Corinne comments], a beautiful, authentic Indian image that I can still see. I felt whisked back. He was taking me into the very center and meaning of that mystic diagram, which in tantric tradition would be fully understood only through visions and spirit guides.

Corinne associates this steak-handed mechanic with her subsidiary Orisha, Agaju, ancient spirit of the volcano. She said that *moving into the meaning of the intricate tantric symbol* was *like falling into the molten center of the earth. That's how I felt.* It is the word made flesh, spirit meatier.

CORA—*The kitchen is aglow with the honey on the table. The wood seems more mellow, the light warmer*, Cora writes. Her note doesn't have far to go, only across the park; but between two busy lives the distance can come to seem formidable. Less so now, though, after we have taken a Veteran's holiday morning to sit at the kitchen table talking of *Oshun and the Psyche*, as Cora puts it. At the far end of Cora's kitchen, a long narrow window is sealed against the November cold. Outside, from time to time the wind howls about the aluminum frame. "Take it easy, Oya!" We acknowledge her presence, like a benevolent ghost, but do not allow her to enter our conversation.

Cora is Brazilian, from the sort of middle-class family that neither condones nor denies the magical world, but rather takes it gently in by osmosis. That Cora's dead grandfather had ap-

peared to some people he had doctored without a fee was cause
of no consternation in her household. Ghosts are unpredictable.
Some see them. Some don't. And when all the machinery—toaster, victrola, sewing machine—in the house mysteriously broke down the same week, Cora's mother logically
asked the servant with whom she felt most comfortable to send
for someone to do the "work" that was needed, which included
a regimen of acrid herbal baths for everyone's protection. After
which, commonsense life proceeded as usual.

Dreamy Cora grew up in a world of forces she feels and locates
in nature as in herself. But here in New York she doesn't talk
about them much. The clinical, academic world in which she
establishes professional identity precludes conversation about
the Orisha. The companionable social world of good food,
music, or watching the ball game with mutual friends dramatizes
Oshun's erotic mission in culture: *to be the glue that keeps it all
together.* Old friends fly in from all over the country to spend a
week, a fortnight in Cora's energetic company; but not many
share the elusive, inner currents that preoccupy the reflective
Cora. These currents solace and at the same time erode the banks
carefully molded to contain them. Cora's conversation ripples
through a thin frame. Sometimes she looks much too tired.

Definition of the word "bagaço." *The sugar cane juice has
been squeezed out. You are left chewing the dry stalk.* This is
Cora's equivalent of Corinne's "dry sponge." *When I am flowing, I am a sweet river. When something goes wrong I am a
drought. Oshun is all about connection—the need to love and
be loved. The flip side of Oshun's need is dependency.* And
dependency fosters vulnerability to betrayal.

Oshun appears in many guises. Her starkest shadow is a bitter
old woman who lives at the bottom of the river. Up to her ears
in mud. *You ring your bell. She rings her bell. She is deaf. She
won't respond. She won't come up. You light a candle on an
outcropping of rock. Somehow, without surfacing, she manages to damp it out. The core of solitude to which one withdraws as a child can sometimes be perceived as the greatest
betrayal of all.*

I know something now about that bitter rage attendant upon frustration of love, the exploitation of dependency. It was important for me to find words for these developmental deficits. The words with which Cora explains herself are drawn from psychodynamic—or, more properly, endopsychic—theory as elaborated in particular by Cora's favorite, W. R. D. Fairbairn. The images with which she illustrates her story are pulled from the family photograph album. The photographs, placed one by one upon the smooth surface of the kitchen table, as though upon a common memory, flicker with life. *The depth of feeling in my grandfather's eyes, his asymmetrical face. I remember being called to spend time in his bedroom. I remember the light in that room. . . .*

My younger sister was born when I was eighteen months old. She developed asthma. So my mother wasn't available. I see myself literally crawling after her. Here's my Nanny. That face. I thought of Frida Kahlo's painting called "My Nurse and I," with its milk-white plant-veins turning to lace on the hem of the grownup-faced infant's slip. *When I was three we had to move to São Paolo, and so I lost the two persons, grandfather and Nanny, who meant everything to me. My father couldn't have cared less. He favored my sisters, who were outgoing. I became depressed. I fled underground, eventually turned to books, developed a false self. But a fantasy took shape inside of me. A sustaining fantasy. I was going to find love. A flawless, beautiful love would prove my worth.* Cora's first marriage was a mistake. *I was still living underground.* Her second marriage is like a carefully tended garden. There are rocks, one supposes, there are weeds. But there are also the tools of diligence. *Oshun. I first saw her face in a ceremony in Bahia. The woman's ample, serene face reflected the pinks and golds of her costume. An immense longing arose in me. Later I recognized this longing. I thought, This is my Nanny. That face clicked in with something hidden inside of me—a real capacity to love and be loved. Yet candomble is a disenfranchised system of belief,* Cora maintains. *It has no words for what I have experienced.* Nor can the language of "inner objects," I maintain, account for the numinous, intimate presence of Oshun and Babaluaiye in Cora's life. We grope for a common language. *I recognize the complex that is Oshun, the complex that is Babaluaiye. I talk to them. "So, you're here today."*

Cora's interpretation of Babaluaiye, her secondary Orisha, is fascinating. The spirit is always represented by a masked figure. The mask is not a face but rather a full veil made of raffia strands (in Brazil) or strips of palm frond (in Africa). According to myth, what is being covered by this veil is, variously, skin disease (Babaluaiye controls smallpox), or madness, or on more universal terms the terrible suffering of the wounded healer, whose flip side, as Cora would say, is lethal sorcery, Death itself. Cora associates Babaluaiye with that primal fear of disintegration which, though we keep it well covered, we continually rediscover through the process of projective identification. Something frightening inside the person sitting opposite in therapeutic space causes a trembling of the veil inside us. *How deep it is down here in the dark. You don't want to see the fragmenting face of fear.* But there it is. My knees turn to water on the path. There have been times when I've had to grip an imaginary cane.

Separation. Abandonment. Though words from a well-enfranchised system of psychiatric credence have brought relief from otherwise inexplicable sorrows, longings, and trepidations, the energy to flow, to connect, and the moral courage to face rage, face fear—those qualities enabling Cora to be doctor of the poor in the rundown veterans' hospital where she works—are infusions of Orisha which Cora feels herself dispensing in the quiet intimacy of supervising others' cases. I had never thought of the assuaging power of supervision in that light before now, though I have been its grateful recipient. *I live it out. It is a daily thing.*

When Cora takes the Type Indicator test from Oshun's point of view, she relinquishes a passion for order and discipline, against which a part of herself rages, only to provoke another part retributively to reinforce. These days Cora is under great pressure to complete her dissertation proposal under conditions exasperatingly bureaucratic and distanced. (She had to make an appointment three months in advance to see her advisor!) One senses the *father who never paid any attention to me but whose standards were stressfully exacting.* This is not how Oshun wishes Cora to live. Go with the flow. If you won't, then I will, ripples the goddess, as Cora struggles to define a cogent research program in the face of faceless authorities in the field from which intuitive connections, that Cora makes so well, are *ab initio* excluded. At this time of professional strain, Oshun withdraws her face from the endopsychic backwaters and swims out into the relational stream.

Cora dreams of men playing football under water. In slow motion their plays are dolphin-like. She dreams of her husband making love to another woman, who could be herself cut loose from anxious, departmental moorings.

Oshun of our mythologies charms everyone into participation, even savage, lonely Ogun, who defines himself by separation from everybody. A folktale recalls how in a time of dearth and danger Oshun persuaded Ogun to forge tools for the rest of us—our use, our protection. The one tool Ogun crafted especially for Oshun was a golden needle with which to sew the fabric of society together. If we're not in the mood, if we're out of sorts, or trying to focus our attention on paperwork, Oshun may seem bossy. It was Ogun who entered Cora's life with a labor-saving computer. Oshun was a bit miffed. So now she's putting Cora in a double bind. And why not? The gods can be cruel. But they alone in binding hold the lifeline that can save us.

Writing of Oshun in two voices. The kitchen comes again aglow with honey reflecting on the scrubbed table. The wood seems more mellow, the light warmer. It's like playing duets on an inner piano. Upstate, the deep snow recedes, uncovering a fall afternoon. The wicker chairs on the patch of lawn outside the kitchen door have been set to catch the golden sunlight. The wind stirs, dislodging here and there golden handprints from a neighboring sassafras tree. The chairs veer round. The conversation continues.

CLARA—*It was much easier to answer Ogun,* Clara reported over the telephone. *I could allow him a simplicity, a directness with regard to thinking and feeling that I wouldn't permit*

myself. I could let Ogun lead from his head, whereas I would always be suspicious that feeling wasn't sufficiently present in my answers. The gods are more consistent. More specifically, *Ogun's in a state of war. He can't afford to let second thoughts take over.*

Clara's Ogun is a mediator, a master strategist, the one who makes sure he has a sure grasp of the facts before acting. No clumsy bushwhacker: the road he clears for his children goes right to the point. He's also the vehicle that gets them there. With Ogun's help you can win a place in the world. But at what cost? *The wounding of the self that is the price of social identity.* This last phrase sounds like a leitmotif throughout Clara's writing both of Ogun in the context of Haitian belief and of her own experience as a successful academic. Having lived for years in a state of war, Clara discovered Ogun at the very time when her wounds were becoming intolerable, yet necessarily borne because the push for tenure was on, and how could she retreat now with this dark epauletted swordsman consciously beside her, urging her forward?

I have known Clara for quite a time, but it wasn't until her writing on Ogun got me to imagining what his presence in her inner life must be like that I could begin to understand the rough edges along which our friendship always threatened to founder. The rough edges were scars, to which, since Clara always seemed to have everything going for her, I had remained obstinately oblivious. Ogun is a terribly difficult Orisha, more painful to assimilate even than Oya, who is, after all, a feminine being, able to insinuate herself, albeit briefly, into contrary situations sideways. Through cracks in the wall. Not head on. Head on is Ogun's fate. And he arrives. Further, Oya is chaotic, always taking off and coming back from a different angle when you least expect her. Ogun, by contrast, is always where he is, is iron.

Antecedent to Ogun's personifications as god of war and patron of hunters is that of divine smith—the one who forged the first tools and weapons. Even more primary is Ogun's identity with the ore itself. "God of Iron" is the first epithet uttered when praising him in Yoruba. The god is also virtually present in his metonymic sacrificial knife. Ogun's knife performs animal sacrifices to all the gods. Without sacrifice, focused in ritual upon the release of blood, there can be no reciprocal release of spiritual energy. Such is the pervasive African belief. Furthermore, and less drastically, within the recognized pain of the cut springs renewed vitality. All of us bear Knife's scars. The lines on our palms brand us as thieves of life.[4] So far, our lot is common. But Ogun also presides over ceremonies of differentiation. Facial scarification in Africa bears witness to tribal identity, circumcision to sexual identity. One is cut in the company of one's peers. Over the bonding which takes place among males who have come of age together Ogun also presides. The excising of women with Ogun's knife is painful to write about because here the hidden or not so hidden agenda is to remove options of sexual pleasure in a polygamous society geared to the production of children in male lineage lines. Traditional poetry compares all these operations of the knife to those of the hoe upon fallow soil. Cultivation and acculturation carry a similar load in our language.[5]

Coming of age and into her own right was a battle from the word "go" for Clara. *I was a rebellious child, uncomfortable with attitudes that were false.* Where was the truth which had to fight so hard against the pressures of conformity? Clara began *to study hard.* When good results failed to win paternal approval, Clara went on to excel. On "career day" in junior high school, Clara tried her mettle by choosing mechanical engineer and astronaut as professional ideals. "But those jobs are for boys," the teacher pontificated. "Not necessarily," said Clara. She dismisses these choices as reflections of what was considered prestigious where and when she was growing up. To which I retort, But Clara, already those were Ogun-choices. Losing interest, however, as time wore on, in materials under stress and pragmatic results, Clara took off into an obtuser zone of philosophical discourse, where one would think gender made no difference. Wrong. Prestigious though the *Critique of Pure Reason* and the *Phenomenology of Mind* were in those days, they were in fact texts written by men for men to interpret to their mostly male graduate students. Nonetheless, Clara kept on. Suddenly, at the top of the dean's list, she realized she was bored.

By great good luck she was offered a job chaperoning students on a study trip to the Caribbean. Suddenly, here was an opportunity to learn about the world through sense impressions. Here were real grounds for spirited inner dialogue with Western thought. Here, patently, was that "otherness" she had felt in herself but lacked the purchase to confront while cruising with increasing facility along the abstract road from Konigsberg to Jena. Throwing philosophy to the winds, Clara became (again, an outstanding) anthropologist and feminist.

"Otherness." Here lodged that truth which had had to struggle so long and hard against the pressures of conformity. Simone de Beauvoir's resolute placing of woman in this condition of being, together with ethnography's mandate to hear and faithfully to represent "the other," *marked the beginning of an ongoing conversation with myself as "other." It is a dialogue between my socially created self (the one that is familiar, public, recognized, and rewarded) and the real or potential me. This "other" is also the person I encounter who has a different culture, a different set of assumptions about the world.* It is not simply that Clara's own "other" gets easily in tune with this person outside the pale of Western culture. Beyond empathy, this person, known in anthropological parlance as "my informant," becomes Clara's *current most significant other.* By dislodging this term, "significant other," from its usual psychoanalytic context and relocating it rather ambiguously in a fieldwork setting, Clara accomplishes the sort of syncope between being and doing that contemporary feminist scholars and critics strive for in a variety of ways. (Present company not excluded.)

After six years' fieldwork centered in one Haitian community, Clara *took the risk of submitting my own life to the Vodu system of interpretation and healing.* When she had problems, she asked for readings and took the prescribed ritual baths. Then she went further, and further. Renouncing for good and all a negative childhood experience, or so Clara and I would tend to construe this facet of the story, she chose rebirth into the spiritual community she continues devotedly to study. The gifted, temperamental, earthy priestess about whom this community revolves plays a role in Clara's new life similar to that of

Cora's long-lost Nanny. Except that this Haitian woman is present, willing, and able to accept the projection; whereas Cora's consoling early-childhood memory dissolves into the face of Oshun, the goddess.

But as Plato said, where there's otherness, there's got to be sameness too. The psyches of Clara and her "current significant other" overlap in complicated ways. They share spirits. This woman carries Ogun too. She also carries Dambala, the great serpent (of whom more later). Within their very different professional milieux, they play equivalent roles. Both educate and sustain their students/relatives and clients. As Clara is invited to serve on panels, participate in colloquia, lecture at neighboring universities, so the Haitian priestess is called to cope with the full range of human problems within the restricted immigrant community she inhabits and even beyond. Ogun pulls them both out of themselves to share what they know and elucidate the paths of others.

Where, then, to locate the real "me" of Clara? With them? or with us? Like the bushwhacking, knife-wielding god who made it all possible, the inner Clara stands at some remove, tirelessly guarding a double frontier. She writes of *the aliveness felt in the presence of the "other"* and of the insight that such contact brings. But since it is awareness rather than fusion that Clara's soul is used to, *the clarity and the energy come in the moment when I pull back from the primacy of experience and stand in the current of fresh air that pulses gently through the crack between our worlds.* Alone on the steel-girdered bridge between the Haitian community she permitted to initiate her and the professional world into which she fiercely (as any woman must) initiated herself, Ogun is with her. Is this such a bad place to be?

There is a further point to be made about Ogun's sword. It was the Haitian community who immediately recognized the aura of Ogun about Clara's head. *It came as a complete surprise to me.* But watching Ogun perform in the ceremonies, Clara came face to face with how her own anger works. After Ogun has chased around wielding his sword in the direction of supposed enemies, the compass of his action narrows to those close at hand; and then in a climactic gesture he bends its tip toward his own heart. There where the rage began it can only come home to roost. There's no other place.

I believe it would be a mistake in a feminist critique of war to paint women as only nurturers, only creative. (Similarly), *I feel it can be dangerous to attribute only goodness and light to the realm of the spirit.* (I believe) *a greater danger lies in not acknowledging that part of the spirit, that part of the human community, and that part of my own psyche which are anger-filled and war-making. I prefer to name it, to own it, and from that place to work to transform it.*

But how? Upon the graph of the Type Indicator test, Ogun can be seen leading Clara way out along the practical survival paths to leadership, knowledge, and self-command. To transform anger one would have to follow the contrary route—trusting in things unseen, relinquishing preconceived ideas to fortuitousness of the moment. Or so it seems to me, hardly to be trusted in this regard, for look where Oya leads her unwary votary.

"I feel such a bond growing up among the four of us Orisha-possessed women" was what I said to Clara the night we sat by the fire and talked all this out. "The two Oshuns, who have never met, enjoy thinking of each other out there." *"It's a bond of the mind only,"* said Clara, *"and of your Oya-mind in particular. You can't turn in need to that sort of community . . ."* ". . . which like the chameleon feeds on air," I laughed. Touché, Ogun. No, an intuited community of kindred spirits can't hug you long distance, can't fix you a hot cup of coffee when you're feeling out of sorts. Nor can it root you—unless you happen to be an aerial plant. What Clara wants is the equivalent of blood lines, of family.

Well, she has it, potentially, by way of Dambala, her auxiliary spirit, to whom she was also ritually married. *At the time, this marriage meant more to me in a sensuous, feeling way* than what in effect was but ratification of a lifelong liaison with Ogun. But Clara has never written about this other exchange of rings, partly because the experience was too close to the skin to be expressed in words, partly because its implications are still on the way to being realized. Dambala, great rainbow serpent, is the most ancient of the vodu spirits to possess people. The flow of his benevolence and his ancestral wisdom are articulated in that most beautiful of ritual dances, the Yanvalu, during whose course a community of undulating bodies glides along feelingly. You have to get way down to do the Yanvalu. You have to isolate and move in harmony six separate parts of the body as your feet creep along without leaving the ground. This same dance expresses the motion of Agwe, king of the sea. Dambala couldn't possibly take the Type Indicator test because he cannot articulate himself verbally. He's too deep for that. But in his wake may be found reconciliation.

CAROL—As though it were a new patent medicine, she had to take it herself before prescribing it to others. Taken fast with Oya, the test was fun. No second thoughts. Simply nailing down one yes/no alternative after the other. Convinced that these pure impulses would end up describing a meaningful arc, Carol let the goddess have her head. Just this once. It's always that way with Oya, just this once. *But that's a mistake*, said Clara, gently, over the telephone. *I once heard somebody say you've got to learn to ride the horse in the direction it's going.* "You're right. For months now I've been far too conscious of the bit in her mouth," said Carol. "I myself placed it there. No wonder she hasn't been speaking freely to me. This paper, for example. For weeks it just sat in a doldrum unable to figure out how to proceed with itself. And if Oya won't think for me, nobody will. Just look at the test results." *Don't sit*, said Clara, *I can't bear to think of you that way. If you must be still, hover.* Like a copter. Blades cutting the air.

"It's all there in writing," Carol went on, "but I have never really applied what I've said about Her to the me-nobody-knows." *They don't know you,* Clara consoled, *because whatever you have to say is dense, obscure, of necessity indirect.* "You mean nobody can see it, but only its effect." *Yes,* laughed Clara, *you're always writing the wind. Which doesn't invalidate what you're doing. It's just that you can't expect the obvious rewards.*

Cora sends Carol an Afro-Brazilian folk saying on a postcard: *A alma e um sopro A alma e um vento.*

Soul is a puff, a blast, subsiding to a rumor—the merest suggestion by a hidden prompter. Soul is breath. Staring at the juxtaposed graphs generated by the Type Indicator, Carol was amazed to see how short-winded and compensatory her "me" had become. Everything tended toward the mean. Like a character in one of Oliver Sacks's vignettes, Carol had taken to wearing spirit-level glasses in order to right her balance; and in the process she was becoming more and more myopic.

Oya brings you out of yourself, said Cora. *She opens you up. She gets you making cognitive maps.* Her patterns in nature are like that, always flowing in spirals. But it's not easy to read them. Overcharged, they cry for adaptors.

Thanks for coming to see us, writes Corinne. *The questionnaire got me to thinking. It's going to take time to dig deeper to find the non-physical aspects that involve Oshun and me on a true core level, to get to what's there in essence, not just its manifestation or incarnation.* Thanks for writing that, thinks Carol, for affirming your stance. Helps to keep me honest. Yet in your dreams flesh and spirit meet, gilding your wings, giving you lien on property.

To each of us the Orisha concedes a little toward the fit. Recently, Carol has been entertaining the possibility of the gods as numinous neurotransmitters, keying into the highly specific human beings each of us is, thus triggering off gradual personality changes and transforming awareness. Into some of our locked selves Oshun can manage to fit a key. Or Ogun or Oya or another spirit may turn out to be preemptive owner of our hidden real estate. Which does not preclude subsequent sharing of the field. It is the opening gesture that is crucial, irrevocable, and forever worthy of the deepest homage.[6] But if polarities govern the world, then it makes sense after a while to begin to differentiate: another locked or fenced off part, another spirit entering. That we can perceive the continuous drama and labor to provide it with provisional form allows us to become less passive toward destiny. The story being written is not strictly speaking ours, for we're but thieves of life, of Others. Yet we pretend it is.

Reprise

Orisha Oshun at the moment is focusing on being a container for Corinne, so that she can mend and reconstitute her personality in a safe, loving matrix. But She is also leading her feelings out into the world of people and places. Within Cora's psychic field, Oshun continues to mitigate academic pressure by speaking of love and affective relationship, while Babaluaiye—hidden god of suffering—connects her deeply with the clinical work she does in the hospital. Ogun, artificer, carries the weight of Clara's professional accomplishment, with its resulting scars, and permits another part of Clara, sinuous Dambala, to intuit more harmonious currents flowing between herself and companions of the moment. And Carol vows without animus to wing it with the gusty impertinence of her rational function. For it was that mode of Oya which got her out of the doldrums and on to the page to begin hazarding connections between enslaved, centrifugal parts of herself in African religious context.

Without the creative participation of Corinne, Cora, and Clara, no inquiry along these lines would have happened. It was a study necessitating the creation of Carol as a fourth "character," not more privileged than the others, and in certain ways weaker. The fictive form which developed naturally out of the task at hand answers to the need for polyphonic writing in the human sciences generally. As the up-and-coming generation of reflexive anthropologists has pointed out, an objective report of the Other's way of going about the business of living and perceiving is no longer possible. Similarly, we can no longer justify an omniscient psychoanalytical voice reporting others' dreams and life histories. Even when there are extensive quotations from crucial therapeutic sessions, these, especially if summarized, are by mode of presentation distorted. The interlarded interpretive passages are, after all, uttered by but one voice —suspicious in its authoritative tone. Analysis, we are fond of saying, is interactional. Each client is capable of bringing into sudden relief some countertransferential fragment of our always only partially resolved complexes. Why then conceal the dramatic irony? Why not present ourselves too as contextually other than we are? Why not leave a space in the script for client to reflect back upon experienced stages of engagement with the protean analyst?

And always one imagines an unheard conversation going on between whatever daimones, gods or spirits of the place and persons involved. Since it's perfectly possible that the thematic emphasis taken by each participant in our study has as much to do with where the investigator's intersected with hers as with meditative self-interpretation, to posit a concurrent metadialogue, sometimes sweet, sometimes stormy, going on between Oshun and Oya and between Oya and Ogun places a value on the collaboration which is truer to the way we felt about it than could be expressed by our own improvising and responding voices as depicted upon these pages.

Yet, imperfect though they be, how else than by such exchanges on earth can we come to know what we are? It is a madman, the Yoruba say, who dances alone without the drum. At least, the rhythms our hidden selves compose their thoughts to being mutually intelligible, we are closer to a broader definition of the person, even in Western parlance, than we were before.

Appendix I: "As Though My Orisha Took the Test"
Myers-Briggs Type Indicator Report

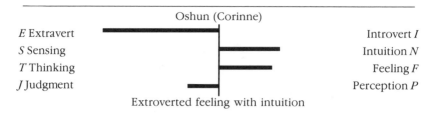

Oshun (Corinne)

E Extravert	Introvert *I*
S Sensing	Intuition *N*
T Thinking	Feeling *F*
J Judgment	Perception *P*

Extroverted feeling with intuition

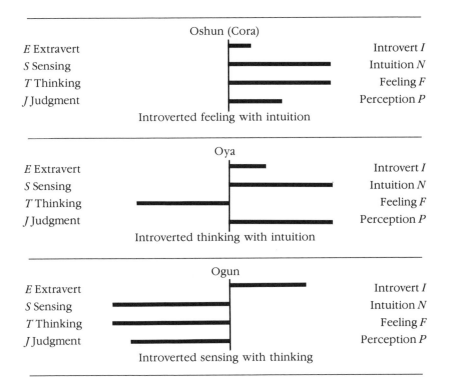

Oshun (Cora)

E Extravert	Introvert *I*
S Sensing	Intuition *N*
T Thinking	Feeling *F*
J Judgment	Perception *P*

Introverted feeling with intuition

Oya

E Extravert	Introvert *I*
S Sensing	Intuition *N*
T Thinking	Feeling *F*
J Judgment	Perception *P*

Introverted thinking with intuition

Ogun

E Extravert	Introvert *I*
S Sensing	Intuition *N*
T Thinking	Feeling *F*
J Judgment	Perception *P*

Introverted sensing with thinking

Appendix II: "I Myself Am Taking the Test"
Myers-Briggs Type Indicator Report

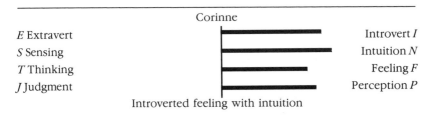

Corinne

E Extravert	Introvert *I*
S Sensing	Intuition *N*
T Thinking	Feeling *F*
J Judgment	Perception *P*

Introverted feeling with intuition

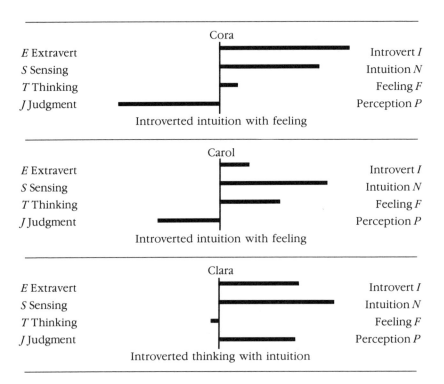

Cora

E Extravert	Introvert *I*
S Sensing	Intuition *N*
T Thinking	Feeling *F*
J Judgment	Perception *P*

Introverted intuition with feeling

Carol

E Extravert	Introvert *I*
S Sensing	Intuition *N*
T Thinking	Feeling *F*
J Judgment	Perception *P*

Introverted intuition with feeling

Clara

E Extravert	Introvert *I*
S Sensing	Intuition *N*
T Thinking	Feeling *F*
J Judgment	Perception *P*

Introverted thinking with intuition

1. All the women's names are fictitious. Here and there some biographical details have been slightly altered to protect professional identities. For rhetorical reasons as well, the interviews have the air of fiction about them. In order to convey a sense of personal uniqueness (external manifestation of the individuation process), I have respected their own styles of conceiving the project and taken their emphases where they put them. Thus, I didn't ask Corinne about her childhood because she didn't bring it up. Or, it didn't come up. Therefore it is not at this time the issue. Cora's voice inevitably reaches beyond the confines of her section because she helped me interpret the test results. Of course, as any *aficionada* of the religion would point out, this outreach is "very Oshun." Clara has written extensively on her experience of the Haitian gods. Therefore, some materials of discussion were present before we began to talk, even if this talk created its own focus, a focus determined in part by our intersecting issues. My intellectual sense of Ogun, derived from oral traditions of the Yoruba, allows a certain freedom of dialogue with Clara's experiential Ogun on the archetypal level of implication. But however on or wide of the mark my interpretation, snatches of everyone's own words, set in italics and coterminous with those of the narrator, set the tone and provide the leitmotifs for each section.

2.   To one of the women who participated in this study, a secondary Orisha is indispensable as guide in her vocation and as an organizing image of what her discipline calls "pre-Oedipal" issues. It would have been interesting to have asked this hidden god to take the test as well. Talking to Cora about her conception of Babaluaiye—Yoruba representation of the wounded healer archetype—I was led to connect him to recent eruptions of primal fears of my own. In another instance it was the reverse situation. Having spent countless hours learning the dance appropriate to Clara's secondary spirit, when she spoke of her initial reactions to him in ritual context, I could imagine his future importance as a balancing element in her life story.

3.   This is the sheet which covered her during initiatory seclusion. One is advised to keep this sheet apart and to wrap oneself in it at times of sickness.

4.   Ifa oracle, "Ogbe Ika."

5.   Ibid.

6.   Such words are patently evocative of the clandestine loyalties women maintain toward their first lovers. If the deflowering was sociopathic —incestuous, or brutal rape by strangers—the psyche preserves a self-wounding "fidelity" to this unspeakable pattern.

FROM MIRROR TO WINDOW
Curing Psychoanalysis of Its Narcissism

JAMES HILLMAN

> ... the apparently individual conflict of the pa-
> tient is revealed as a universal conflict of his en-
> vironment and epoch. Neurosis is thus nothing
> less than an individual attempt, however unsuc-
> cessful, to solve a universal problem. ...
>
> C. G. Jung, *CW* 7, §438 (1912)

I.

Narcissism is now the rage, the universal diagnosis. In Freud's world, the new attention was on conversion hysteria; in Bleuler's, dementia praecox. Earlier we find all ills attributed to the English malady, to spleen, to hypochondriasis, to melancholia, to chlorosis; in Paris, a myriad of *phobies* and *delires.* Different times and places, different syndromes.

Narcissism has its theoreticians—Kohut, Kernberg, Lacan —and modern Jungians are following the rage. The collective consciousness of psychology makes us collectively unconscious, much as Jung said when writing about the collective ideas in his day. Being "with it" also means being in it. The epidemic diagnosis "narcissism" states that the condition is already endemic to the psychology that makes the diagnosis. It sees narcissism because it sees narcissistically. So let us not take this diagnosis so literally, but place it within the historical parade of Western diagnoses.

Eminent culture critics—Thomas Szasz, Philip Rieff, Christopher Lasch, Paul Zweig, and the notorious Dr. Jeffrey Masson—have each seen that psychoanalysis breeds a narcissistic subjectivism inflicting on the culture an iatrogenic disorder, that is, a disease brought by the methods of the doctors who would cure it.

I shall continue their line of thought, but I shall use a method that Wolfgang Giegerich has so brilliantly exposed in many of his papers. If depth psychology itself suffers from a narcissistic disorder, then what we analysts need first to probe is the unconscious narcissism in analysis itself. Our first patient is neither the patient nor ourselves, but the phenomenon called "analysis" that has brought us both to the consulting room.

The term "narcissism" is probably British. Havelock Ellis is credited with its invention, though Freud gave us its psychoanalytic meaning. What did Freud say? As I go through some of his descriptions, let us hear them narcissistically, as self-referents, descriptive of psychology and of ourselves in psychology.

1917: "We employ the term narcissism in relation to little children and it is to excessive narcissism of primitive man that we ascribe his belief in the omnipotence of his thoughts and consequent attempts to influence the course of events in the outer world by magical practices." Does not analysis have this primitive omnipotence fantasy of influencing events in the outer world by its magical practices? The omnipotence of subjective reflection is attested to by many classic Jungians like Harding, Bernhard, Meier, von Franz, Baumann, etc. As Jung himself says, we are each makeweights in the scales that determine the outcome of world history (*CW* 10, §§586–88). The rituals of self-engagement remove projections from the world so that, supposedly, the world itself is transformed by psychoanalysis.

1922: ". . . narcissistic disorders are characterized by a withdrawal of the libido from objects." *The withdrawal of the libido from objects*—I ask you to remember this statement. We shall come back to it.

1925: Freud describes three historic blows to humankind's narcissism. These, he says, are the cosmological blow of Copernicus, the blow of Darwinian evolution theory, and the psychoanalytic blow (of Freud) which wounded the omnipotence fantasy, or narcissism, of the ego as sole self-willed ruler. Here, psychoanalysis becomes itself a giant omnipotence fantasy, a creation myth of our culture equivalent with astronomy and biology, promulgating itself with narcissistic grandeur.

This pronouncement appears in Freud's paper on "Resistance to Psychoanalysis." By means of this idea, resistance, analysis brilliantly maintains its invulnerability to criticism. Intention to doubt the validity of analysis is impugned as resistance to it. Even more: the very attacks demonstrate resistance and therefore help to validate analytical theory. As Freud says (1928, "Humour," *CP*, 5: 216), ". . . the triumph of narcissism, the ego's victorious assertion of its own invulnerability. It refuses to be hurt by the arrows of reality. . . . It insists that it is impervious to wounds dealt by the outside world. . . ."

Later, Freud considered narcissism not to be rooted in love at all, i.e., as self-love, but to be rather a defense against aggressive impulses. Let us consider a moment the value of "aggressive impulses"; at least and at best they take the object, the world out there, into account: I feel enraged about societal injustice, nuclear danger, media crap, industrial callousness, the corporate mind, political ideologues, hideous architecture, etc. But, owing to my narcissistic defenses against the involving call of aggression, I go to the spa, work out, meditate, jog, diet, reduce stress, relax my body armor, improve my orgasms, get a new hairstyle and take a vacation. And—see my therapist: very expensive, very good for me, because he or she devotes complete attention to my problems, especially our transferential frame. Instead of the world and my outrage, I work on my analysis, myself, the Self. This Self, too, fits a narcissistic definition: "the incorporation of grandiose object images as defense against anxiety and guilt" (Lasch, 36) or, as Fenichel (1945, 40) puts it, one feels oneself in "reunion with an omnipotent force," be that force an archetype, a God or Goddess, the *unus mundus*, or the numinosity of analysis itself.

Freud's paper "On Narcissism" (1914, 52–54) states that both introspection and conscience or "being watched" derive from and serve narcissism. Yet, psychotherapy practices self-scrutiny as the principal method in its treatment and "being watched" or supervision as the principal component of its training. A candidate goes to hour after hour of institutionalized narcissism of watching and being watched.

The institutionalization of narcissism in our profession—in the idea of resistance, the idealization of the Self, in the practices of introspection and supervision, in the omnipotence fantasies about its own importance in world history, in its technique of referring all events back to itself as the vessel, the mirror, the *temenos*, the frame—bears immediately upon that central obsession of analysis today, transference.

II.

By transference, here, I mean that self-gratifying analytical habit which refers the emotions of life to the analysis. Transference habitually deflects object libido, that is, love for anything outside analysis, into a narcissistic reflection upon analysis. We feed analysis with life. The mirror that walks down the road of life (Flaubert) replaces the actual road, and the mirror no longer reflects the world, only the walking companions. They may as well have stayed at home, less distracted by the trees and the traffic.

The principal content of analytical reflection or transference is the child we once were, a fact which accords with Freud's observation that the object choice of the narcissist is "someone he once was" (1914, 58). This helps account for the faddish popularity of Alice Miller's writings. Her idealized children exhibit what Freud said: the narcissist is "not willing to forego his narcissistic perfection in his childhood" and "seeks to recover the early perfection" (ibid., 51). The focus on childhood traps the libido only further into subjectivity, and therefore we must recognize that erotic compulsions in analysis are produced primarily by the analysis, rather than by the persons. Analysis acts itself out through them quite impersonally so that they often feel betrayed and ashamed by the impersonality of the emotions they undergo and are unable to recognize that what they are suffering is the object libido trying to find a way out of analysis. Instead, the narcissistic viciousness of our theory says that transference emotions are compelling the persons to go deeper into analysis.

Let us recognize that the other person—patient or analyst— embodies the only possibility within an analysis to whom object libido can flow. The person in the other chair represents cure of analytical narcissism simply by being there as an Other. Moreover, the patient for the analyst and the analyst for the patient become such numinous objects because they have also been tabooed as libidinal possibilities. Analyst and patient may not act their desire for each other. The narcissism of the *situation* makes them absolutely necessary to each other, while the taboo sets them absolutely outside of each other. This outside object, however, is also inside the analysis. So, patient for doctor and doctor for patient become the symbolic mode of ending analysis by means of love.

Of course, the persons are often torn by what Freud calls "the love dilemma of the narcissistic patient: cure by love rather than cure by analysis" (1914, 59). We must ask, however, whether this neurotic choice, as Freud calls it, arises from the narcissism of the patient or from the narcissism of the analytical system in which the patient is situated. After all, the fantasy of an opposition between love and analysis occurs within the prior fantasy of cure which has brought the persons together in the first place.

By elaborating ethical codes, malpractice insurance, investigations and expulsions which blame the participants, analysis protects itself from wounding insights about its own narcissism. The vulnerability of analysis—that its effectiveness is always in question, that it is neither science nor medicine, that it is aging into professional mediocrity and may have lost its soul to power years ago despite its idealized language of growth and creativity (a language, by the way, never used by its founders)—this vulnerability is overcome by idealizing the transference.

As well as transference love, there is also hatred. Perhaps the client's hatred of the analyst and the hatred of the analyst for the client are also not personal. Perhaps, these intense oppressive feelings against each other arise in both to present both with the fact that they are in a hateful situation: the object libido hates the attachment of transference. Analysis hates itself in order to break the narcissistic vessel imprisoning the libido that would go out into the soul in the world.

The horned dilemmas of transference, including the analyst's stare into the mirror of his own counter-transference, the feelings of love and hatred, this agony and ecstasy and romantic torture convince the participants that what is going on is of intense importance: first, because these phenomena are expected by the theory and provide proof of it, and second, because these phenomena re-enact what analysis once was in its own childhood in Vienna and Zürich, analysis in primary fusion with its origins in Breuer and Freud and Jung, in Dora and Anna and Sabina. The feelings are cast in therapeutic guise because this is the healing fiction of the analytic situation. In other words, transference is less necessary to the doctor and the patient than it is to analysis by means of which it intensifies its narcissistic idealization, staying in love with itself. We do not sit in our chambers so many hours a day only for the money, or the power, but because we are addicted to analytical narcissism. Our individual narcissism is both obscured and reinforced by the approved narcissism of the analytical profession.

When one partner imagines a tryst or the other imagines resisting a seduction, or when either imagines that love is a solution to misery, then they are framed in the romantic conflicts of *Madame Bovary, Wuthering Heights,* and *Anna Karenina,* reconstituting the Romanticism of the nineteenth century and the origins of psychoanalysis, not in your or my personal childhoods, but in its own cultural childhood. This means we have to locate the narcissism of contemporary analysis within a much wider narcissism: the Romantic Movement.

III.

Literary tradition differentiates at least four principal traits of
this genre. We have already spoken of one: "idealization of the
love object." And indeed analysis idealizes the patient as an "interesting case," "difficult patient," "good patient," "borderline
personality." Or consider all the literary fabulations that have
made patients into eternal literary figures—Dora, Ellen West,
Babette, Miss Miller, Wolfman, Ratman, Little Hans, all the way
to Freud and Jung themselves in the novels *The White Hotel* and
The House of Glass. Think of the Romanticism in our theoretical
constructs—Love and Death, Empathy, Transformation, Growth,
The Child, The Great Mother, The Mirror, Desire and *Jouissance.*
In the patient there takes place such idealized events as a *hieros
gamos,* a quest for self-discovery and a journey into wholeness,
synchronicities outside of causal laws, transcendent functions,
integration of the shadow and the realization of the Self on
whom the future of civilization depends. We record our idealization of the love object, i.e., analysis, in taped and filmed analytic
sessions, paying meticulous and expensive attention to trivial
conversations and gestures. Analysis is in love with its idealized
image.

A second essential trait of Romanticism is said to be the opposition between bourgeois society and the inner self which,
with its dreams, desires and inspirations, tends to oppose, even
contradict, the outer world of usual things. Psychoanalysis from
its beginnings imagines itself fundamentally opposed to the
civilization and its institutions of religion, family, medicine, and
the political community disdained as "the collective." Freud's
emphasis on himself as Jew and hence marginal, as well as Jung's
favorite position as heretical old hermit (despite the bourgeois
lives they led and values they held), still shapes the imagination
of the profession and distorts its relation to the ordinary world.

Third, imprisonment, another basic theme in Romanticism,
especially French and Russian. In Dostoevsky's *The Possessed,*
Maria's song says: "This tiny cell suffices me, there I will dwell
my soul to save." The consulting room provides the confining

physical place for the psychic imprisonment of analysis as such: its devotion to the secret nooks and crannies of the private world, decorating with reconstructive rococo (i.e., psychodynamic intricacies) the narcissistic cell of personality.

Fourth, the Romantic genre has been defined as one that simultaneously seeks and postpones a particular end. This fits therapy. Its entire procedure seeks to restore the person to the world, yet postpones this return indefinitely. (Meanwhile, do not make major changes in your actual life. Don't act out. The cure of analysis becomes more analysis—another analyst, another school—and the improvement of training becomes ever more hours.) The simultaneity of seeking and postponing an end occurs in the basic conundrum of every analysis, its contradictory two commandments: encourage the desires of the unconscious (Thou Shalt Not Repress) and forbid gratification (Thou Shalt Not Act Out). Our work is with the libidinous and our method is by way of abstention. The end is unforeseeable; there is no completion. Analysis interminable, as Freud said. This is the Romanticism of eternal longing.

There is no way out of Romanticism's consulting room and the subjectivism of its eros, unless we turn to what is beyond its purview, turn to what narcissism and romanticism leave out: the objects, the unidealized, immediately given, actual world of dull and urban things. By turning psychological attention from the mirror of self-reflection to the world through the window, we release "object libido" to seek its goal beyond narcissistic confinement in analysis. For "object libido" is but a psychoanalytic name for the drive which loves the world, the erotic desire for *anima mundi*, for soul in the world.

Perhaps it becomes clearer why I have been emphasizing John Keats's remarkable phrase: "Call the world . . . The vale of Soulmaking. Then you will find out the use of the world. . . ." Also, you will understand why I have held myself back from that side of Jung which expounds upon meaning, Self, individuation, *unus mundus,* wholeness, mandalas, etc. These large and introverted ideas envelop me and usually my patients with a grandiose, invulnerable aura. As well, I keep a distance from the current Kohut craze. Although recognizing narcissism as the syndrome of the times (even if the groundwork for this was prepared long ago in the metaphysical catastrophe of Augustinian and Cartesian subjectivism), yet Kohut attempts its cure by the same means of narcissistic obsession: an ever more detailed observation of subjectivity. And—a subjectivity within the oppressive confines of a negatively reconstructed childhood. The child archetype dominates contemporary therapy, keeping patients (and analysts) safe from the world. For this archetype feels always endangered by the actual world, lives not in the present but in futurity, and is addicted to its own powerless infantilism. By so focusing on the child, analysis disenfranchises itself from the wider realm of soul-making in the adult community of *polis*.

Nevertheless, I must confess to a serious longstanding error on my part regarding Keats's phrase. I always considered the world out there to be useful for making one's own soul. Narcissism again. My soul, your soul—not its soul. For the Romantics, however, ensouling the world itself was a crucial part of their program. They recognized the traps of narcissistic subjectivity in their vision. Hence, they sought the spirit in physical nature, the brotherhood of all mankind or *Gemeinschaftsgefuehl*, political revolution, and a return to the classic Gods and Goddesses, attempting to revivify the soul of the world with pantheism.

We must therefore read Keats as saying, we go through the world for the sake of *its* soul-making, thereby our own. This reading suggests a true object libido, beyond narcissism, in keeping with Otto Fenichel's definition of love. Love can only be called such when "one's own satisfaction is impossible without satisfying the object too." If the world is not satisfied by our going through it, no matter how much beauty and pleasure our souls may receive from it, then we live in its vale without love.

IV.

There is a way out, else I wouldn't be standing here. For my specific style of narcissism, my pose before the mirror, today is heroic. My style insists on resolution of the issues raised. The method I shall be using here follows the method which I usually employ for resolving issues. First, we look back into the history of psychoanalysis for a model; second, we turn to some peculiar bit of pathologizing for a clue; and third, we resolve problems by dissolving them into images and metaphors.

So, let us turn back to the first psychoanalytic case, Anna O., and her doctor, Josef Breuer, who, with Freud, wrote *Studies in Hysteria.* As you recall, after a year of almost daily sessions often of several hours, he suddenly terminated. You recall also the intensity of her transference, that she developed a hysterical pregnancy and childbirth, after Breuer tried to end the treatment. He, according to Jones, after a final visit to her "fled the house in a cold sweat. The next day he and his wife left for Venice to spend a second honeymoon which resulted in the conception of a daughter." Whether fact or not, and Ellenberger says not, the fantasy shows a founding patron of our work escaping both cure by analysis and cure by love for the beauty of Venice and the conception of a daughter. His object libido returns from the oppressive narcissism of psychoanalysis to the romanticism of the wider world.

This wide world remains merely that, merely a place of escape or acting out, so long as the world "out the window" is imagined only in the Cartesian model as sheer *res extensa,* only dead matter. To show more vividly how that world is, as Keats said, a place of soul, let us go straight through the window into the world. Let us take a walk in a Japanese garden, in particular the strolling garden, the one with water, hills, trees and flowers. While we walk, let us imagine the garden as an emblem for the peripatetic teacher or the therapeutic guide (psychopompos), *the world itself as psychoanalyst showing us soul,* showing us how to be in it soulfully.

I turn to the garden and to Japan because of insights given while in Kyoto gardens several years ago, and also because the garden as metaphor expresses some of the deepest longings —from Hesperides, to Eden's paradise, and Maria's *hortus inclusus*—for the world as home of the soul. So, by entering into the Japanese garden now we shall be stepping through the window into the *anima mundi.*

First: we notice that the garden has no central place to stand
and view it all. We can but scrutinize a part at a time. Instead of
overview and wholeness, there is perspective and eachness. The
world changes as we move. Here a clump of iris, there a mossy
rock. Instead of a center (with its etymological roots in the
Greek *kentron*, "goad" or "prick," and being compelled toward
a goal by means of abstract geometric distancing), there are
shifts of focus relative to the body's location and attitude.

Second: as one strolls, each vista is seen again from a different
perspective. The maple branching down to the pond edge, the
floating leaves appear less melancholic after the path bends.
These shifts of seeing again are precisely what the word "respect" means. To look again is to "re-spect." Each time we look
at the same thing again, we gain respect for it and add respect to
it, curiously discovering the innate relation of "looks"—of
regarding and being regarded, words in English that refer to
dignity.

Third: when the garden, rather than the dream or the symp-
tom or the unconscious, becomes the *via regia* of psyche, then
we are forced to think anew about the word "in." "In" is the
dominant preposition of all psychoanalysis—not *with,* not
from, not *for,* but "in." We look in our souls, we look in a mirror. "In" has been taken utterly literally, as an invisible, space-
less psychic stuff inside our skins, or the meanings inside our
dreams and symptoms, or the memories locked in the past. Interiority of the garden, however, is wholly present and wholly
displayed. "In" holds the meanings of included, engaged, involved, embraced. Or, as Jung said, the psyche is not in us; we
are in the psyche. This feeling of being in the psyche becomes
most palpable when inside the ruins of a Greek temple, in an
Egyptian tomb of a king, in a dance or a ritual, and in a Japanese
garden. Jung's phrase *"esse in anima"* takes on concreteness
then, as it does also in a clear-cut forest, a bombed city, a cancer
ward, a cemetery. Ecology, architecture, interior design are
other modes of feeling the *anima mundi.* In fact, the relation of
body and psyche reverses. Instead of the usual notion of psyche
in body, the body strolling through the garden is in the psyche.
The world itself is a psychic body; and our bodies as we move,

stand, look, pause, turn, and sit are performing an activity of psychic reflection, an activity we formerly considered only mentally possible in the mirror of introspection. To know oneself in the garden of the world then requires being physically in the world. Where you are reveals who you are.

Fourth: the idea of individuality also changes, for in the Japanese garden trees are trimmed at the top and encouraged to grow sideways. Rather than an individuality of the lone tree, towering (and Jung said the single tree is a major symbol of the individuating Self), these trees stretch their branches toward others. Individuality is within community and takes its definition from community. Furthermore, each tuft in the soft branches of the pine trees is plucked by gardeners. They pull out needles, allowing emptiness to individualize the shape of each twig. It is as if nothing can be individualized unless it is surrounded by emptiness and yet also very, very close to what it is most like. Individuality is therefore more visible within the estranged separateness and close similarity, for instance, of family than in trying to be "different" from family.

Fifth: not only are aged trees supported with crutches and encouraged to flower—blossoming belonging therefore not only to youth—but also the garden includes dead trees. What more wounds our narcissism than these images of old age, these crutched, dependent, twisted and dead trees?

Sixth: the Karesansui gardens, or Zen-inspired gardens, present mainly white sand and found stones, rarely trees. In this bare place the mind watches itself making interpretations. The nine rocks in the raked sand are a tiger family swimming through the sea; the nine rocks are mountain tops peaking through white mist and clouds; the nine rocks are simply rocks, aesthetically placed with genius. One legend after another, one philosophy, theory of literary criticism or psychological interpretation rises to the mind and falls back into the white sand. The garden becomes wholly metaphor, both what it is and what it is not, presence and absence at once. The concrete koan of the rock garden transforms the mind itself into metaphor, its thought transient while image endures, so that the mind cannot identify with its own subjectivism—narcissism overcome.

V.

Finally, I shall insist that the garden is not natural; nor is psyche natural. The garden was designed and is tended to maintain an artificiality that imitates nature. In Fort Worth, Texas, a large and marvelous Japanese garden was constructed years ago. But since funds were not set aside for gardeners from Japan, nature slowly destroys that garden. Without the pruner's perverted twist to each inch of nature, the garden declines into merely another part of the forest. A garden's elaborated display of soul-in-the-world is an *opus contra naturam,* like alchemy. Like alchemy, the garden is a work of intense culture. Unlike alchemy, its matter, its body, is out there, rather than inside the glass vessel.

Because the garden is artificial, as the alchemist was called *artifex,* all conceptions of soul must be plucked of naturalistic fallacies. The soul as *opus contra naturam* will not be served adequately by fallacious comparisons with organic growth, cyclical process, and myths of nature Goddesses. Nor does the garden shelter the child from which grows the creative person as psychotherapy is fond to believe. By insisting upon the artificiality of our work with soul, I am trying to keep us from the Romantic error of confusing the ideal (Eden and the Elysian fields; Horaiko, in Japanese) with the natural. The garden as metaphor offers a romantic vision that saves us from Naturalistic Romanticism, by twisting and sophisticating nature through art.

This twist to nature that wounds idealizations of garden is presented in our culture, as in Roman culture, by our ancient God of gardens and gardeners, Priapus. Priapus is neither young nor beautiful. Unlike lovely Narcissus, unlike the semi-divine figures of Adam and Eve, Priapus is mature, bald and paunchy, and so distorted that his mother, Venus, deserted him at birth. His very presence repels romantic idealizations and the gaze into the mirror of Venusian vanity as well as Narcissus's rapt reflection. Priapic reflection starts the other way around; his preposterous swollen condition reflects the vitality of the world. The same force displays in him as in the buds and germinating pods. By means of distortion which deceptively seems "only natural,"

Priapus invites the grotesque pathologized disproportions of imagination—and imagination, says Bachelard, works by deformation.

So, when I invoke Priapus, I am *not* speaking of priapismus; I am not speaking of *machismo;* and I am not anti-feminine. Let me be quite clear. I am speaking of the generative artificiality that is the essence of the garden and of the psyche. Each dream, each fantasy and each symptomatic complication of natural health and normative humanity bears witness to the psyche's libidinal pleasure in exaggeration, its fertile genius for imaginative distortion. If this God of gardens is also a God of psychoanalysis—and from Charcot through Lacan the priapic has been invoked—he brings to its work an archaic reflex beyond the romantic or baroque, a rousing urgency forward and outward. (Priapus was not permitted indoors in Hestia's closed rooms where his presence becomes only violent and obscene.)

Moreover, this God needs no mirror to know himself, for his self is wholly displayed. His nature cannot be concealed within, so he is quite free of hidden meanings and subtle innuendos that keep psychoanalysis hopefully addicted to one more revelation, one more transformation, interminable.

> Priapus knows no metamorphosis . . . no transfigurations. . . .
> Priapus is without ambiguity . . . metaphor is forbidden to him
> . . . he displays all, reveals nothing. (Olender, 387)

Like the garden, all there. The rocks are the rocks.

Bibliography

Ellenberger, Henri F. *The Discovery of the Unconscious.* London: Allen Lane, 1970.

Fenichel, Otto. *Psychoanalytic Theory of Neurosis.* New York: Norton, 1945.

Freud, Sigmund. *Collected Papers.* London: Hogarth Press, 1924–.

Hillman, James. "Abandoning the Child." In *Loose Ends*, pp. 5–48. Dallas: Spring Publications, 1975.

Kerényi, Karl, and Jung, C. G. "The Myth of the Divine Child." In *Introduction to a Science of Mythology.* London: Routledge & Kegan Paul, 1951.

Olender, Maurice. "Priape le mal taillé." In *Corps des Dieux.* Paris: Gallimard, 1986 (translation mine).

PAN'S "THEATRE OF THE WORLD"
Notes on "Object-Metaphor"

ENRIQUE PARDO

The Cuban poet José Lezama-Lima suggests that every object aspires to a colossal dimension that, rather than having to do with size, is imaginal, where it can "reach its figuration, triumph over formlessness." "A superior mode of excess, a new creative configuration of men and gods."[1] This could be said to be the aim of Pantheatre's "object-metaphor" work: to realize the colossal figuration of the object-world, to bring Pan back to life in the rocks, bushes and objects that moaned and mourned the announcement of the god's death, and their reduction to "dead matter." Through this "colossal" and "panic" work, both actor and spectator work on object-related, "objective" emotion.

In the *Timaeus* (34c), Plato describes the world as an animal that has a body, a soul and an intellect. In Timaeus's words, the creator-god put soul at the center of the universe and then extended it throughout and beyond its confines, as a sky enveloping it. World, anima and animal are overlapping categories in Plato's cosmogony. Our language only differentiates the words "anima" and "animal" by the tail-end of the letter "l". One can hear in the Platonic interplay of these two words that the objects of the world are animals with a soul; that imagination is the animal in the object; that image-making is soul speaking in the world. These are extrapolations that I try to root through object-metaphor work. The actor seeking out imagination enters into an animal rapport with objects; the animal in him will sense the anima in matter; this implies animal moves, animal receptivity. Such an approach to the "theatre of the world" is an education of the "instinct of image," the animal helping us to converse with the colossal soul of the world.

The cosmogony that Plato lays out in the *Timaeus* is followed by a whole section of detailed formulas, of measured combinations of how to dose, mix, blend, compound, compress, suspend, synthesize "nous" and "soma" (all these are his terms). Theatre image-making is a microcosmic reflection of this Platonic "haute cuisine." It brings together "nous" as the breath of poetry, the world of ideas, with physical, visual and vocal matter. It kneads them together in an architecture of fusions, tensions and openings where imagination coagulates.

The French ethnographer Jean Bazin has recently published an article titled "Retour aux choses-dieux" (Return to the things-gods).[2] The article is based on what are called "bolis": conglomerates of objects used by the Bambara tribes from Mali. In specific ceremonies, bolis are placed in earthenware and sprayed with the blood of animals killed by an officiant. Bazin defines the aim of his article (one could speak here of the "object" of his article) as follows: "I simply want to question the nature, the ontological status of these things: I try to have some idea of what happens when they are thus sprayed with blood."

Bazin uses neither the word "soul" nor "imagination," and his article is precisely about the danger of projecting our Western notions of "soul" and "imagination," through so-called scientific observation, on such ceremonies and cult-objects as the Bambaras' bolis. By calling on Heidegger—his essays on things and thingness—and contemporary French post-modern criticism, Bazin enhances the status of these bolis and demonstrates how they have been diminished by being associated with the derogatory connotations of notions like fetishism, idolatry and animism. He disentangles and in a sense delivers these objects from our Western moralized rational fear of imagination, and of its ambivalent polysemic potential.

I have often spoken harshly of what I have referred to as "anthropological esthetics" in theatre. By this I refer to the excessive veneration paid to exotic non-Western rituals and to the model of the shaman in the imagination of acting, models that come mainly from the credentials of anthropology. Anthropology combines the fascination of exotic and reputedly authentic religious phenomena with the detachment of scientific observation. If I here call on Jean Bazin's article, it is precisely because of the way in which he questions his own field and the lenses it has used to serve and to fascinate itself.

The notion of fetishism turns imagination into a religious pathology; the fetish thing, by being turned into a replacement idol, loses its autonomous imaginal identity, its thing-ness. According to Bazin, one does not ask a boli "what do you represent?" In itself a boli is seen as a singular object, a thing-god. A boli is not a symbol re-presenting a god or a genius hidden somewhere in the bushes. Nor is it a tabernacle enclosing a hidden or invisible being. These are speculations that come out of the observers' spirit/matter dichotomy. The "symbolic" and the "tabernacle" approaches turn out to be the prevalent ones one encounters in theatre object exercises. Actors construct and get caught in scenarios that are based on these premises, like the ethnographers whose theories Bazin deconstructs.

The first question one asks a boli is "what are you made of?" The answer is in sensual perception, in physical engagement. One does not search the object for symbols, but for the immediate images of its material presence. The more a boli acquires a unique, singular status, the more "god" it is. Similarly in object-metaphor work: the more an actor recognizes and respects the individual thingness of the object, the more in touch he comes with its soul. Imagination rises from the detailed perception of the object's singularity, its texture, patina, articulation, location, scars, awkwardness, its character and the tangible memory it has accrued on itself. Such an encounter moves imagination. The actor then deploys the object's colossal figuration; he is moved by its will. When this occurs, object and image are one, in the same manner that Bazin says that thing and god are one, and the onlooker perceives its metaphorical power or mana and is "showered by a rain of metaphors."

Bazin actually speaks of the "process of individuation" of a boli—of how it acquires individual god nature: "the principle that presides over its production is of individuation, not of representation. . . ." It is a question of "constantly engendering a new singular body" (264), of becoming a "thing-person" (266).

The process of spilling blood onto the boli is central to the individuation process. According to Bazin, the sacrificial model does not apply to these ceremonies, since the blood is not offered to an absent or represented deity. The blood directly enhances the presence of the object which gets "charged, so to speak, with enormous metaphorical power." Rather than using terms like "transference" or "projection," Bazin suggests that a term like "transfusion" would be more appropriate. Similarly in object-metaphor work: if there is any sense in which the term "sacrifice" can be used, it is in the relinquishing of personal subjective imaginations. As a form of transfer it is an exorcising of the actor's subjectivity by the "thing-god." One offers one's metaphorical blood to it, like to the souls in the Underworld.[3]

With bolis, "we are rather on the side of mystic devotion: the divine is not only felt affectively, but materially manipulated, in the same beatitude of the immediate" (270). Here is another phrase that seems to come straight out of an object-metaphor theatre session! The mechanics of engagement imply setting the object into motion and emotion: waking it up, animating it. Correct engagement is at the heart of this imaginal craft. Bazin reports that, among the Bambara, one does not speak of acquiring or buying a boli, "one marries it" (266)! And to qualify the type of marriage involved, he states that ". . . in no case is it the material mass that is being 'adored,' but a sufficiently complex body so as to be held as more individual than the human ego itself" (266).

But, at this point there is a strong ambivalence about words like "animation," or even more "manipulation." The latter word has strong connotations of cheating, misappropriation, prestidigitation, manufacturing illusion, fake. Similarly, animation can connote Walt Disney or the craft and psychology of masks or puppet work, the latter two being but one aspect of object-metaphor. What I would like to elaborate on, and which links back to my reserves about "anthropological esthetics," is the fact that we are speaking theatre, artifice, fiction, agreed illusion, and not so-called authentic or pure religious phenomena. We are talking of the actor, the "showman in the shaman"[4] or even the charlatan. Furthermore, by describing this work in terms of baroque esthetics, I accentuate its artificial, "synthetic" aspect.

Bazin mentions "mystic devotion" and "beatitude of the immediate," and, no doubt, there is an atmosphere of religiosity in first approaches to object-metaphor exercises. Of necessity, neophytes to this work, in questioning and discovering other dimensions of imagination, do link back, or re-connect, with religious patterns of creation. Yet, since we are in theatre, the trickster and the miraculous are intertwined. The hermetic element is ever present as an awareness of fiction or metaphorical commerce. Irony and play are an integral part of imagination, and, beyond reverential first approaches, the actor enters into a highly complex and ambivalent dialogue with things-gods. Image-making becomes a complicity, often irreverent and sacrilegious, involving even, to paraphrase Bazin, negative transfusions, demystification.

On Technique and Titanic Teachers

Let us now return to the fabulous Neoplatonic philosophies and, more specifically, to the Orphic fables on the dismemberment of Dionysus that so fascinated Proclus. Proclus read the passage on the "anima mundi" that I quoted earlier from the *Timaeus* as Plato's interpretation of the allegedly earlier Orphic tales on Dionysus. In this lineage of thought, which we know to be outside historical logic, imagination speaks through fabulous allegorical spirals. I will further confabulate on these and cast some mytho-poetical light on the technical aspect of "object-metaphor" work. I wish to give the word "technique" a fabulous, soul-making dimension. More than ever, at this point it is necessary to hold together mythological speculation and practical, manual exercising, blood and psyche, fantasy and object.

The Orphic story tells of the dismemberment of the infant

Dionysus by the Titans at the instigation of the goddess Hera. Proclus saw in the scattered members of the god the multiple ubiquity of Plato's "anima mundi," and he saw in the preservation of the infant's heart the soul's unity; the Dionysian heart remained unaffected by the cruelty of the Titans. I associate the Titans with technique: they are the fabulous technicians, the mythical surgeons that operate the dismemberment and scatter soul into the world. Without them, Dionysus, reputed to be the god of theatre, would have remained a baby-god, and imagination would have remained in the crib, identified with the infant, as it remains for so many today. Titanic cruelty tears this baby-imagination apart, boils it, and casts it out into the world. The egocentric, unified imaginal body of the infant is torn into its different components, differentiated. Titans were said to have souls of steel, which fits our image of technique: the hard, arid, steel-like, analytic dissociation drills that actors are put through in "object-metaphor" exercises are a titanic endeavor, tearing apart the infant's subjective vision, its innocent wholesome body, so that it may see the world, and even his own members, as "other." These are exercises that tear movement away from language, separate voice expression from words. They are based on principles of syncopation, counterpoint, differentiation, conversion, often seeking the poetics of contradiction. They frustrate illustration, emphasis, global unified energy, and tear into the fabric of fiction in order to reassemble complex synthetic images. Titanic dissociative techniques are the basic tools toward baroque solutions.

On Deadpan Allegories

To round up this fantasy exegesis on the Orphic Titans, some remarks on the Dionysian heart, on the infant's playpen, and on the role of Hera. There is much to be said about the survival of the heart of Dionysus in these tales and on the reunification of the god by Apollo. I would like to simply point out that, within titanic technology, the heart of the matter must remain alive while the body of theatre is being torn apart. Proclus identifies the "intelligent heart" with Plato's universal intellect. James Hillman devoted a recent Eranos lecture to "The Thought of the Heart." The titanic nature of dismemberment disseminates Dionysian imagination and inseminates the world with soul. Within this process of disjunction, explosion, separation, there must remain at the center a presence of mind that is heartful. The heart irrigates the soul in the world, gives it its *semantic blood*. Without this thoughtful heart, we are in a universe of aleatoric surrealism, meaningless drama, a random cosmogony of imagination. A lot of contemporary theatre is nothing but "deadpan allegories."

A few remarks now on objects as toys, the world as playground. The Titans lure the infant Dionysus through a collection of toy-objects. Titanic dismemberment is preceded by game. Playful animation is a prerequisite to a heartful dismemberment, a stage where objects are caught in the realm of game, a playful soulfulness. Imagination has an infant, animal, playful heart which must precede and survive titanic dismemberment, like the fascinating games that kittens play with woolen balls.

My last remark on this Orphic fantasy pertains to the role of Hera. She commissions the murder, the child's titanic dismemberment. Within this perspective, we encounter the so-called bad stepmother (and Hera has tended to get very bad press from all quarters, from the advocates of family to feminists and artists)—we encounter Hera as the figure behind the maturing, soul-creating titanic operation. Maybe her ruthless cruelty is necessary to break up the Zeus–Dionysus father–infant protective bond, necessary in order to recognize soul in the world. Until one has come to terms with the Titans and the so-called bad mother, one remains an eternal Cinderella, and the "Theatre of the World" will not move out of the infant's playground, a sweet pumpkin fairytale.

On Baroque Giants

The seventeenth-century Spanish Jesuit Baltazar Gracián places the notion of "disenchantment" at the heart of baroque esthetics. Re-ensouling the world, on the other hand, is often referred to as the "re-enchantment" of the world, making the soul in the world sing again. This enthusiastic, romantic tradition of enchantment sees soul in the natural beauty of the world, like Saint Francis talking to the birds and flowers, as paracletic divine manifestations. Gracián's seems to be a fallen, decadent universe, while the Franciscan vision links up with the rediscovery of the soul in the world, the enthusiasm of a re-birth, a Renaissance. These are two seemingly opposite "Theatres of the World." One presents a lively miracle, the other a deadly metaphorism. Both are essential for a full simultaneous apprehension of the baroque notion of imagination that I wish to convey: the conjunction of titanic metaphorical dispossession while keeping intact the enthusiastic, bloodful heart. Baroque images seek the tensions and paradoxes that can contain such abysmal disparities. In the performance "Hercules: Twelve Baroque Labors,"[5] the mythic hero confronts through muscular enthusiasm the theatre of object-metaphor, completely missing the point. The result is both comic and pathetic, for after all he represents our own egos desperately fighting the metaphor of death. Through his heroic failures he allows us a tragic insight into the otherness of the imagination of the world. This baroque Hercules, like the Neapolitan Farnese statue of him, is a heavy, melancholic, depressed figure pondering the futility of his life's labors.

The Farnese Hercules is a baroque giant, like that other figure whose point of view we might profit considering: Goliath. Michelangelo's colossal struggles are the turning point of the Renaissance—his saturnine gigantic efforts exhaust a certain imagination. They weigh down the youthful, enthusiastic Renaissance, of which the figure of David, the young intrepid shepherd boy, is in many ways the emblem. Mannerism and Baroque art turn in titanic compassion to the decadent, heavy, anchoring figures of Goliath and Hercules, to their disenchanted insight. A figure who is literally caught in this dilemma is Calderón de la Barca's Sigismundo, a giant of vitality, imprisoned in the play "Life Is a Dream." From his dark cell, from his torn soul, come some of the most glorious celebrations of nature. I am thinking of the central speech on the freedom of the bird, the fish, the beast, the stream: a song that rises from the heart of baroque disenchantment, where Calderón describes a wild animal, a baroque version of Plato's anima(l)—a daring and cruel beast whose fur markings were painted by divine brush strokes to reflect the constellations of the stars.

1. José Lezama-Lima, "Introducción a un Sistema Poético," in *El Reino de la Imagen* (Venezuela, Biblioteca Ayacucho). My translation.

2. Jean Bazin, "Retour aux choses-dieux," in "Corps des dieux," in *Le temps de la réflexion* 7 (Paris: Gallimard, 1986). My translations.

3. In a recent talk, James Hillman stressed how infernal images seek embodiment—as in the *Odyssey* where the souls of Hades came out seeking blood. They give voices to our fantasies: talking alone aloud.

4. From a lecture by Charles Boer on "The Actor of Trois Frères," normally called the "sorcerer" or "shaman."

5. "Hercules: Twelve Baroque Labors," 1986, a solo performance created with Francois Didier.

"I LOOKED FOR YOU
IN MY CLOSET TONIGHT"
Voyeurs and Victims
in *Blue Velvet*

CYNTHIA J. FUCHS

> We have educated ourselves thoroughly in the
> psychopathology of contemporary art, but we
> will not understand our time until a mind ap-
> pears which can demonstrate the phenomenon
> of the critical mind turning upon itself, fre-
> quently producing a truly hallucinatory quality,
> freakish posturings directly at odds with the
> very process (if we can no longer speak of
> values) it sees itself as promoting. The ideal
> reader has become, like the ideal artist before
> him [*sic*], a kind of monster.
> Charles Newman, *The Post-Modern Aura*

> Maybe I'm sick, but I want to see that again.
> Quoted in *The New Yorker*

> This is all the way America is to me. There's a
> very innocent, naive quality to my life, and
> there's a horror and a sickness as well. It's
> everything.   David Lynch

David Lynch's *Blue Velvet* is a movie for "our time." Released
in late 1986, the film incited various responses from reviewers,
ranging from ecstatic reverie ("An erotic masterpiece") to
outrage and disgust ("the sickest movie ever made"). Here is "a

critical mind turning upon itself," revealing our "postmodern
condition,"[1] our self-contradictions, our monstrousness:
Lynch's vision represents a hallucination and freakishness to
match exactly the time.

But what exactly marks this time as different from another? Is
Lumberton, U.S.A., representative of an American mindscape?
Does *Blue Velvet*, given its depiction of violence and sexuality,
offer any imaginative breathing room for the female viewer? Or
has Lynch represented a psychopathic environment in a way
more insidiously and insistently real than Real?

It happens that *Blue Velvet* was released around the time of
the fortieth birthday of Frank Capra's *It's a Wonderful Life*.
Among the movie-watchers who noted this were Richard Corliss
(who calls the film "the evil twin of *It's a Wonderful Life*")[2] and
Janet Maslin, who included it in a round-up of films that
"rethink the small town" using an innovative and energetic lexicon of images (like David Byrne's *True Stories* and Jonathan
Demme's *Something Wild*).[3]

But as these critics applaud Lynch's athletic (if somewhat sin-
ister) imagination, they resort to an archaic vocabulary,
adopting without question the ready-made binary terms in-
scribed by and in American cultural mythology—the very same
terms that Lynch's film *does* question. According to this general
theoretical dichotomy, the film depicts the hither side of the
picket-fenced suburbs, the evil half of the American Dream.

True to a point, this reading misses the film's other agenda,
under the underside. Lynch offers a glimpse at a complicated
text, the one supporting the glossy American self-image which
reads itself in figures of dark and light, male and female. *Blue
Velvet* begins where the construction of the American daydream
and nightmare no longer governs perception, where nightmare
becomes the waking reality, the spectacle becomes the spectator.
Frank Booth (Dennis Hopper) is at last no aging Mr. Potter who
can be wheeled off-screen at the end of the movie. He has to be
blown off with a gun, and even then he remains, as traces of
music and strains in a narrative unable to circumscribe itself.

Immediately, *Blue Velvet* complicates the relation between
subjective vision and the "objective" represented world by

assaulting visual assumptions, those assumptions that equate "seeing" with "believing." The slightly slow motion of the fireman's wave and the sway of the redder than red flowers indicate a vision shaped by its self-distance, a point of view which simultaneously defines and discredits itself. Normal structures of signification seem untrustworthy: do these too-yellow daffodils mean what they seem?

While outside Mr. Beaumont waters his suburban lawn, inside Mrs. Beaumont fertilizes her suburban imagination by watching a thriller on television. But as soon as it has established the expected duality between a "Leave It to Beaver" daily life and a dark and dangerous fantasy, the film strips its gears and hurtles into another narrative: our diurnal Dad suffers a stroke, and the back yard turns into a threatening psychological food chain. The hose spurts wildly, while Mr. Beaumont clutches the gun nozzle at penis level; a small dog attacks the hissing spray, slow motion emphasizing its vicious leaps over the downed man's body. And the camera takes us down—down into the chthonic world in the green lawn, into a hyper-realized realm where bugs literally chew the scenery.

What is normally invisible to the human eye becomes extraordinarily visible. In revealing film's capacity for distortion and illusion, *Blue Velvet* not only lays bare the technological mechanism of film—which, after all, is not new to viewers used to self-conscious filmmaking—but also the ideological elision of perception and representation. The film exposes the "contradictory work of difference, non-similitude, false repetition which at once found and limit the deception (of cinematic illusion) in order to rethink representation."[4]

Blue Velvet disrupts signifying processes dependent on binary structures. Rather than delineate a real world and an Other world, the film collapses the two, suffuses the one with the other. The film resists integration and resolution, hovering in a movement back and forth from the representable world and that unrepresentable off-space, figured in Lynch's roaring soundtrack and nightmare images of flame and distortion.

In daylight, we come home with Jeffrey Beaumont (Kyle MacLachlan), who returns to mind his father's hardware store (which, according to the film's dark humor, sells axes and chain-saws) while the old man is incapacitated, encased and silenced in tubes and machinery in the hospital. Like his celluloid pred-ecessor, George Bailey in *It's a Wonderful Life*, Jeffrey has had his collegiate context cut out from under him, but unlike George he has no guardian angel to watch over him. Instead he has us, impotent and implicated in the process of watching him.

Jeffrey's plunge into the dark recesses of the bug world begins when he finds an ant-covered human ear "behind our neighbor-hood." The neighborhood proves to be infested with creepy characters and mysterious events—Jeffrey's delusion of safety zones (he tells his Aunt Barbara not to worry because he's "just gonna walk around the neighborhood") soon disintegrates. All signs indicate his folly: the camera pans to the television set where *film noir* feet ascend a stairway just as Jeffrey descends. Outside, a large man in dark glasses looms over his tiny dog (the same one who jumped on Mr. Beaumont?), trees hang ominously over the sidewalk, and teenaged boys accost Sandy (Laura Dern) from their car when she and Jeffrey near the "Deep River Apart-ments," where Dorothy Vallens (Isabella Rossellini) lives. The "Donna Reed" neighborhood is transformed in the dark, seething with repressed evil. Even so, the film clings to the pathological banality and ambiguity of Jeffrey's repeated obser-vation, straight out of "My Three Sons": "It's a strange world."

Sandy puts the movie's central question to Jeffrey this way: "I don't know if you're a detective or a pervert." The problem the movie presents is that things are not clear-cut; instead moral boundaries and power relations have become multiple, fluid, disturbingly indistinct. Because Jeffrey is our narrative and moral point of reference, we observe and absorb his self-doubt, his failing self-image. Linking perception with perversion, the film questions audience "joyrides," guiltless thrills—viewers are held responsible for their visions.

Included in the category "viewers" are the theorists and critics who determine a closed system of reading in which the reader/viewer maintains anonymity and inculpability. *Blue Velvet* can be understood as a critique of film theory's impulse toward what Stephen Heath calls "narrativization," the "reconstruction of the [viewing] subject" within a coherent, linear discourse. This process of identification with an on-screen consciousness allows an ideologically ordained closure by whatever textual acrobatics necessary.[5]

In trying to account for the spectator's absence within the film text (to fill the textual gap), psychoanalytic film theorists have followed the Freudian lead concerning sexual difference and privilege—they assume a male subject. Christian Metz relies on a Freudian/Lacanian model of castration anxiety in formulating the "all-perceiving subject," a paradigmatic spectator who "identifies with himself [*sic*], with himself [*sic*] as a pure act of perception (as wakefulness, alertness): as the condition of possibility of the perceived and hence as a kind of transcendental subject, which comes before every *there is*."[6] Metz's circular construction of the subject is founded on the male child's discovery of the mother's "castration," the infamous scenario whereby the male fear of Lack is conveniently effaced by its projection on the nearest available target, Mom. The female body represents Lack and from there comes to figure unrepresentability. Within this logic, perception and representation form a closed system based on sexual difference, continually reinscribing the binary condition which privileges the male, perceiving self over the unrepresentable female other.[7]

Blue Velvet, like Hitchcock's *Rear Window* (1954) and Michael Powell's *Peeping Tom* (1960), addresses the troubled relation between subjectivity and perception (figured in film's "highly dispersed" enunciation), undermining the illusion of an authoritative vision.[8] Ostensibly taking the conventional male point of view—the youthful hero of a film noir plot who gains knowledge and vision through experience—the film makes problematic what Metz calls "transcendental" subjectivity by subverting the hierarchical structures supporting this illusory power of perception. In doing so, the film opens a place for female viewers within a male-dominated economy of gazes.

We look with Jeffrey but also see him looking. Our voyeuristic vehicle Jeffrey explains his and our fascination with the object Dorothy: "I'm seeing something that was always hidden. I'm involved in a mystery. I'm in the middle of a mystery."

Diegetically, that "mystery" is Frank's bizarre relationship with Dorothy; implicitly, it is another side of the American 'burbs and of Jeffrey himself, what Metz might term a "pure act of perception."

The meta-narrative mystery starts where the hierarchy of viewer and spectacle, male and female, collapses, where it becomes possible to "conceive difference without opposition."[9] Similarities among the characters collide, differences dissolve, no matter their gender or generic roles. And distances separating spectator from spectacle cease to be safe. It's no longer only the center that won't hold, but cultural boundaries as well that fail in the uproar, the postmodern "loss of mastery."[10]

Appearances dissemble. Jeffrey's prototypical love interest emerges, quite literally, from the night's same threatening darkness: "Are you the one who found the ear?", Sandy asks, establishing an intimacy based in a forbidden text, the circular depths of the ear leading to destruction and decadence beyond normal language and experience. While her father serves as the more socializing of Jeffrey's "father" figures (the other being the rampantly a-social Frank), Sandy serves as his source of information and inspiration. A "mystery" to the unsuspecting Jeffrey, in her most obvious incarnation she is the idealized girl-woman who lives next door and dates a football player.

Sandy figures Jeffrey's own flip side too—his George Bailey-esque return to Mary and Marriage. She is loyal and game for his schemes, posing as a Jehovah's Witness to his Bug Man to help him explore Dorothy's apartment. "There are opportunities in life," he intones over a hamburger at Arlene's, "for gaining knowledge and experience. Sometimes it's necessary to take a risk." Sandy's "risk" involves setting up and falling in love with a potential pervert, and then watching his investigation. The film limits her perspective, forcing her reliance on second-hand information: she "sees" via Jeffrey; she only knows "bits and pieces"; she represents our unreliable and impaired vision.

Significantly, Sandy's moment center stage is the description of her parodic "dream." While the church organ swells and the stained glass windows glitter, Sandy (in the driver's seat for the first and only time) rhapsodizes about the hundreds of robins bringing "the blinding light of love" to the world (it's better not to see). "You're a neat girl," exults George cum Jeffrey. And next to Frank, she seems "neat" indeed. Her depthlessness reflects that shallow daylight part of Jeffrey, the part of the American psyche that the movies seem condemned to reify. Her curiosity encourages his narration—she is the perfect reader for the binary-plot.

Or again, Sandy is the daylight to Dorothy's nightlife place in Jeffrey's storyline. Threatened by a careening car while driving Sandy home, Jeffrey mistakes Mike (Sandy's boyfriend) for Frank (Dorothy's abuser). This misidentification marks the conflation of his multiple existences, a slip brought on by Jeffrey's violation of male proprietary rights in two realms. Mike's narrative correspondence to Frank (and their similar impulses to exact damages through violence) parallels the male prerogatives and anxieties which dictate high school courtship and sado-masochistic rituals. Mike's boyish attack is goaded by his drunkenness. Frank's is enhanced by his gas-mask.

At stake in both confrontations are the women's bodies. Sandy's long and lithe body, revealed in close-fitting sundresses, poses an ideal far different from Dorothy's more "realistic," out-of-shape lumpiness. Both bodies are marked as distinctively other, objects of (Jeffrey's) gaze. He/we watch Dorothy get undressed; he/we see Sandy finish dressing for their date. Seemingly true to form, the film establishes the dark-haired Dorothy as the sexual object and the blonde Sandy as Jeffrey's "chaste" love object.[11]

Even as it sets up stereotypes, however, *Blue Velvet* breaks down the cultural types and assumptions of women, particularly in the scene where Jeffrey spies on Dorothy in her apartment. Here the relationship between spectator and spectacle is not so polarized, especially in a postmodern context, where "subject" no longer makes up a definable thing. And just as the "subject" cannot be limited to a cohesive consciousness, neither can the "object" be seen as a passive thing for a controlling gaze.

Dorothy is first a performer. At the seedy "Slow Club," she is

"The Blue Lady," singing only songs that have the word "blue" in the title, bathed in a blue spotlight. She appears the projection of the many male gazes directed at her, including Jeffrey's.[12] In her apartment, she performs again, for the unseen Jeffrey. Stripping to her underwear, the Blue Lady is revealed as an artificial spectacle. Dorothy's imperfect naked body, while not literally "grotesque," connotes a transgression of cultural ideals, especially since she becomes an object of desire for the designated "normal" man, Jeffrey. Her makeup, cheap wig, and exotic costume mark his entrance into a world of vice and masquerade, where appearances don't signify.[13]

When the phone rings, she immediately flattens herself against the wall at attention and responds with (apparently) rehearsed lines: "Yes, sir," "Mommy love you." Her performance for another unseen audience links Jeffrey (and us) with the terrorist caller.[14] Dorothy's role as the object of an aggressive gaze (Jeffrey's, Frank's, ours) limits her as a construction of (male-defined) female sexuality, a cultural product.

But again the terms change: Dorothy's discovery of Jeffrey in the closet does more than reverse their positions. Her interrogation of Jeffrey confuses the established spectator–spectacle relation:

"What's your name?"
"Jeffrey."
"Jeffrey! Jeffrey what?"
"Jeffrey nothing."
(Reading his wallet identification) "What are you doing in my apartment, Jeffrey Beaumont?"
"I wanted to see you."
"Get undressed. I want to see *you*."

Jeffrey's insistence on his anonymity as a spectator incites her violent response. She pricks his cheek with a knife, violating the safe distance between viewer and viewed. Kneeling before him, she orders him to strip, makes him approach her ("Come closer!"), and then fondles him, threatening to kill him if he looks at her. Her performance here is aggressive and violent.

Only after Frank arrives are we aware of the extreme irony of the preceding sequence. Dorothy's command—"Don't look at me"—resonates when we realize its source is Frank. Within the balance of performance and spectatorship, looking implies power for the subject over the object. In taking control of the order of "looking," Dorothy usurps the traditional male role.

Minutes later this shifting equation unravels. Frank's entrance and Jeffrey's resumed voyeurism lead to a perverse re-staging of Freud's "primal scene," with Frank alternating between "father" and "baby" to Dorothy's "mother."[15] Raw, rough, and unredeemed, Frank explodes on the scene and in his pants, representing the violent and sexually aggressive patriarchy gone wild.[16] The violence of Frank's favorite obscenity—"fuck"—is sexual but in his language is directed at anything "other." He vows to "fuck anything that moves."

Frank's excess is pornographic, "the limit-case of acceptable discourse," destroying the possibility for regained narrative stability but allowing Jeffrey (at least temporarily) to define his moral stance in opposition to it.[17] What is not "pornographic" in the scene, however (why the film received an "R" rating), is the absence of "the graphic display" of Dorothy's body parts.[18] The film focuses on the violator rather than the violation, at once underlining Jeffrey's (our) identification with Frank and the ravishing look. Frank's mastery and Dorothy's submission are based in his exclusive control of the look, furtively mediated at this point by Jeffrey's and our compulsive watching.

The violation of Dorothy is multiple, the camera alternating between Jeffrey's horrified response and the scene he can't not watch. Encoded with viewer dis-ease and distress, the scene does not allow narrative distancing, regulation and enclosure; instead, it enforces our responsibility for "lawless seeing."[19] Jeffrey's "looking" in the sado-masochistic ritual is later underlined by his physical reenactment of it: in bed with Dorothy, he hits her (in slow motion and twice, so there can be no mistaking his intentions), mirroring Frank's action and accompanied by the roar on the soundtrack that marks Frank.

Jeffrey's sexual relationship with Dorothy is conditioned by the violent, violating terms under which he meets her, as well as the masochism she has assimilated from her relationship with Frank. Both of their "dates" (following the first night) are prefaced by "dates" with Sandy. But where Sandy resists Jeffrey's kiss (because she loves Mike), Dorothy embraces him and leads him to her bedroom (while the camera rests on the billowing curtains in the front room). When Dorothy pleads with him to "hurt me," Jeffrey counters with "No. I want to help you." But in Dorothy's vocabulary, the two are synonymous. "Hurting" is pleasurable and sex is destructive: Jeffrey and Frank are her interchangeable abusers. Though Frank's act of "intercourse" is more malignant, less conventional, than Jeffrey's, Dorothy draws a connection, telling Jeffrey, "I have your disease in me now."

Frank names his relation to Jeffrey during the "joyride" to Ben's (Dean Stockwell's) place "Pussy Heaven." The "party" at Ben's parallels and comments on the later high school party where Jeffrey and Sandy exchange vows of love. Ben's violence replaces teenage passion. Behind the closed door are Dorothy's kidnapped husband and child (both named Don); outside are overweight matrons and a bearded man, who seem vaguely threatening in their lethargy but comically outrageous in their anomaly. Ben's horror lies in his lack of definition (his assault on Jeffrey is unexpected), his endless performance, and ultimately his femininity. Cool, druggy, and unnerving, Ben soothes the near-hysterical Frank with pills and "entertainment." His lip-synched version of "In Dreams" parodies and complements Dorothy's renditions of other Golden Oldies and looks forward to Frank's own recital. Ben's grotesque makeup is highlighted by the mechanic's bulb he uses as a "microphone" (as is Dorothy's by the light of her bathroom).

As a figure of masquerade and confusion, Ben represents the border of irrationality Jeffrey crosses in acknowledging his intimacy with Frank. On the one hand, Ben, the film's de-centered focus of "carnivalesque" disruption, means meaninglessness. He refers as well to the (disintegration of the) central opposition which organizes meaning in the narrative and in cultural relations—sexual difference. His ruffled shirt, pasty makeup, and glittery jacket signal his unnatural (and therefore threatening) divergence from the masculine "norm," while not offering the titillating visual uncertainty of female impersonation. Inasmuch as he is constructed as an obviously male but female-like "object of fetishistic looking," Ben still threatens male hegemony through unstable gender identity.[20] Even as we laugh at Ben's ridiculous act ("the candy-colored clown," indeed), he terrorizes.

Frank's transgressions are more severe and easier to name. His own self-styled duality—the well-dressed man disguise—allows him free movement in and out of the two realms he straddles ("normal" corruption in tandem with the police and more obscure, unlimited corruption that he practices with Dorothy and, finally, Jeffrey). Initially a victim of violence by Frank's gang ("He's *our* pussy"), Jeffrey is wedded to Frank by night's end by virtue of their exchange of looks. Frank stops the car when he catches Dorothy looking at Jeffrey ("What does he have to do with anything?"). As Jeffrey stares in horror, Frank demands, "What are you looking at, fuck?" "Nothing," Jeffrey answers, echoing his response to Dorothy earlier. "You're like me," hisses Frank, describing a relation until now articulated only in Jeffrey's recurring nightmares.

Once again, Jeffrey can't not look, his eyes locked on Frank's torture of Dorothy in the front seat. He responds with force at last, and it's like a mating call to Frank. Their mutual violence excites Frank, and the ritual coupling commences. Now Frank orders Jeffrey to "Look at me," asserting their similarity, their mirror imagery of each other. Frank smears his own lips with Dorothy's red lipstick and kisses Jeffrey thoroughly, violently, on the mouth. Both resemble the "clown" of the song "In Dreams," playing in the background. Frank's use of a flashlight under his face recalls Ben's performance of the same song. But its previous implicit disruptiveness is now overt. "In dreams, you're mine," Frank snarls. "If you get a love letter from me, fucker, you're fucked forever." While this appropriation of pop music is horrifically comic, it is also to the point in describing Frank's vision of sexuality as furious exercise of power. A "love letter" is a "bullet," an ejaculation, a show of superior force.

This is no simple case of male bonding, though. At issue here, for Jeffrey and for us, is the conflict among his multiple existences, the relations which define and redefine limits. Both the moral, social world (the place inhabited by Sandy, who takes responsibility for "getting [Jeffrey] into this") and the external, uncontrolled world (Dorothy's repeated plea for abuse) marginalize women in trying to contain them. And the woman dancing on the top of Frank's car while he terrorizes Jeffrey provides more than just comic relief. With her slow motion bumping and grinding (her "freakish posturing"[21]), the dancer hyper-ritualizes and parodies the culture of sex she describes and promotes. She is the flip side of Frank. Like Frank she is a "kind of monster" who no longer represents herself but the processes that create her, contextualize her, contain her.

The "disease" in Dorothy refers to the "technology of sex" which has determined her performances in life, on stage, on screen in *Blue Velvet*. Finally, of course, it is that "disease" which has resulted in Donny, her son, who is returned to her in the film's "happy ending." But as with the opening, the final images are strange, unreal. All families are intact: Jeffrey's solution of the "mystery," his unmasking of Frank's disguise and the corruption of the "yellow man" (Detective Williams's partner), and the restoration of Dorothy to motherhood all seem to lend themselves to the narrative closure and comfort of a Hollywood ending. But look again. The "intact" family has been parodied throughout the film, the robin is mechanical, Dorothy's reunion with Donny is in slow motion and accompanied on the soundtrack by her voice singing "Blue Velvet": "And I still can see blue velvet through my tears." Partial vision, perhaps, but Dorothy's ability to see is painful (as her last look off camera and outside the narrative frame indicates). Throughout, *Blue Velvet* has worked to undermine all the privilege of appearance and vision it has simultaneously underlined.

"Rather than looking at the spectacle of attacks, let us turn this look that isn't ours, elsewhere, and let it see. Let it see both what it was looking at before and us."[22] By turning this "look" around, *Blue Velvet* has broadened its vision to include the multiple "us" as well as the culture that determines who looks and who is looked at.

1. Jean-Francois Lyotard, *The Postmodern Condition: A Report on Knowledge,* tr. Geoff Bennington and Brian Massumi (Minneapolis: University of Minnesota Press, 1984).

2. Richard Corliss, "Our Town: George Bailey Meets 'True,' 'Blue,' and 'Peggy Sue,'" *Film Comment* 22, no. 6 (Nov.–Dec. 1986): 12.

3. Janet Maslin, "New Films Rethink the Small Town," *New York Times,* 21 Dec. 1986, Arts and Leisure, p. 1.

4. See Jean-Louis Comolli, "Machines of the Visible," in *The Cinematic Apparatus,* ed. Teresa de Lauretis and Stephen Heath (New York: St. Martin's Press, 1985), 141.

5. Stephen Heath, "Narrative Space," in *Questions of Cinema* (Bloomington: Indiana University Press, 1981), 54.

6. Christian Metz, *The Imaginary Signifier: Psychoanalysis and the Cinema,* trans. Celia Britton, Annwyl Williams, Ben Brewster, and Alfred Guzzetti (Bloomington: Indiana University Press, 1982), 48–49.

7. Teresa de Lauretis notes that the essential gap in psychoanalysis as a useful theoretical construct is that it always "defines woman in relation to man, from within the same frame of reference and with the analytical categories elaborated to account for the psychosocial development of the male" (*Technologies of Gender: Essays on Theory, Film, and Fiction* [Bloomington: Indiana University Press, 1987], 20).

8. Kaja Silverman, *The Acoustic Mirror: The Female Voice in Psychoanalysis and Cinema* (Bloomington: Indiana University Press, 1988), 12.

9. Craig Owens, "The Discourse of Others: Feminists and Postmodernism," in *The Anti-Aesthetic: Essays on Postmodern Culture,* ed. Hal Foster (Port Townsend, Wash.: Bay Press, 1983), 62.

10. Ibid., 67.

11. Jonathan Demme's *Something Wild* offers another dissection of the Hollywood bad and good women in its conflation of the two in one character: Lulu/Audrey (Melanie Griffith) appears alternately and then simultaneously as dark and light, active and passive. The complication in Demme's scheme is that the initial script, which is Lulu's, reverts to the object of her "look" (Charlie Driggs [Jeff Daniels]), (re-)inscribing her as object in the conventional narrative which takes over the original.

12. Again the relation is problematic: Jeffrey's "typical" wide-eyed response to Dorothy's "erotic" performance is multiply defined by our watching Sandy watch him; by distancing us from his male perspective, the film turns the "look" around on itself.

13. Mary Russo, "Female Grotesques: Carnival and Theory," in *Feminist Studies/Critical Studies,* ed. Teresa de Lauretis (Bloomington: Indiana University Press, 1986), 213–29. Russo takes her paradigm of the transgressive, teasing, seductive "grotesque" from M. M. Bakhtin's theory of the "carnivalesque."

14. Isabella Rossellini describes her role as follows: "I saw a woman who was totally victimized, who has lost all her rationality, who is only emotions." In Laurie Winer, "Isabella Rossellini Assesses the Role That Haunted Her," *New York Times,* 23 Nov. 1986, p. 1.

15. Later Jeffrey's nightmare splices distorted images of his father and Frank.

16.   David Lynch: "I don't know where Frank Booth came from. He just appeared to me one day. There's nobody that I based anything on. For me, he's an American archetype. He's a guy I somehow know from small towns. He's an American heavy. He has to be American, and he has to come from either a desert small town or a Midwestern small town. And he just started talking, and I started writing" (Chris Hodenfield, "Citizen Hopper," *Film Comment* 22, no. 6 [Nov.–Dec. 1986]: 64).

17.   Jonathan Elmer, "The Exciting Conflict: The Rhetoric of Pornography and Anti-Pornography," *Cultural Critique* 8 (Winter 1987–88): 46.

18.   Elmer writes, "Pornography is a representational practice in which women, for all the graphic display of their body parts, are the excluded term." Ibid., 48.

19.   Annette Kuhn, "Lawless Seeing," in *The Power of the Image: Essays on Representation and Sexuality* (London: Routledge & Kegan Paul, 1985), 19–47.

20.   Kuhn, "Sexual Disguise and the Cinema," in *The Power of the Image*, 73.

21.   Charles Newman, *The Post-Modern Aura: The Act of Fiction in an Age of Inflation* (Evanston: Northwestern University Press, 1985), 122.

22.   Catherine Clement, "The Guilty One," in Helene Cixous and Catherine Clement, *The Newly Born Woman*, tr. Betsy Wing (Minneapolis: University of Minnesota Press, 1986), 57.

THE LAST TEMPTATION
AND THE UNKNOWN GOD

JAY LIVERNOIS

No film over the last year has caused as much controversy as Martin Scorsese's *The Last Temptation of Christ*. When it opened in city cinemas around the United States, hundreds, sometimes thousands, of Christians came to picket the film. As a result the movie received more than its share of reviews, discussion, and publicity. But all too often small town movie theaters refused to show it. They were afraid of violent reactions by local Christians, so the film was not easily seen outside major cities, and then many cinemas did not let it run for long. Even in Paris, the world capital of movie theaters, only two film houses agreed to run it. One was almost immediately burnt down by Christian terrorists, and the other showed the film but had to withstand the occasional tear gas canister set off during the movie by Christians in the audience.

The Last Temptation is based on the novel by the Greek writer Nikos Kazantzakis. The bug in the film (also in the book), which has driven Christians to denounce and attack it, is that Jesus is portrayed as a man who has sex with women, specifically with Mary Magdalene and the sisters Mary and Martha. It seems the fantasy that Jesus could have had sex, and that he was not an otherworldly male virgin, is intolerable to contemporary Christians.

This intolerance of sexuality is not found in the Gospels, as nowhere in them is it said that Jesus was a virgin or celibate or even unmarried. In fact the New Testament strongly hints at Jesus' sexual interests.[1] For example, he breaks Jewish religious laws by eating on the sabbath with sinners, he is familiar with prostitutes and protects adulterers from stonings (because of sympathy or interest?), and critics have long assumed that he had sexual relations with Mary Magdalene, Mary of Bethany,[2] and/or with the obscure Salome.[3] Some commentators have even speculated that Mary Magdalene was Jesus' wife.[4]

It has also been thought that Jesus had a homosexual attachment to the disciple John (who was possibly the same person as Lazarus?),[5] the disciple "whom he loved." While sodomy was of course a Jewish taboo, homosexuality was not unusual in Palestine and was accepted throughout the rest of the ancient world as but another form of eros. Furthermore, the Jesus who freely broke most of the Jewish laws and religious taboos as part of his radical vision may have found this repressive side of the culture particularly useful to his revolution.

In recent years, Morton Smith, the noted New Testament scholar, has shown how Jesus had "secret teachings" for his disciples which were essentially Chaldean erotic (probably homoerotic) magical rites.[6] Smith shows conclusively that during the "Passion" in the garden of Gethsemane, when Judas betrayed Jesus and he was arrested, Jesus was practicing one of these rites. The rite was "a special baptism," a magical initiation into "the kingdom of heaven." Smith shows how this explains the otherwise bizarre scene found in the account of the "Passion" in Mark where a young man in a linen cloth (the same cloth used in ancient magical initiation ceremonies and to shroud the dead) is with Jesus as he is arrested in the garden but runs away naked leaving his garment behind when the Temple police try to seize him.[7] "And there followed him a certain young man, having a linen cloth cast about his naked body; and the young men laid hold on him: And he left the linen cloth, and fled from them naked" (Mark 14:51–52).[8]

None of this is shown or hinted at in *The Last Temptation*. Instead, Satan, in the form of a little girl, tempts Jesus with the idea of giving up the Crucifixion and his sense of being the son of

God, to go on living life as a normal man. Scorsese, in his Catholic schema of things, has Jesus imagine all this on the Cross because, of course, as God's son, he is omniscient and more powerful than Satan. In this fantasy, he marries Mary Magdalene, who then dies in childbirth. In his despair at the Magdalene's death, Jesus meets and lives with the sisters Mary and Martha in a blissful if boring triangle, having children with both women. The movie fantasy continues until the children are grown, Mary and Martha are old, and Jesus is old and dying. At Jesus' death bed he is visited by the disillusioned disciples, his brother James, and Paul, who blame him for giving up martyrdom for a temporal existence. Jesus' selfish sex life has of course taken away all the heroic possibilities for their lives. At this point in the movie, the little girl reveals herself as Satan, and as Jesus' fantasy bursts he is projected back dying on the Cross. He has resisted domesticity, after all, for his religious mission and death. So the movie ends.

More than Jesus' sexuality, what *The Last Temptation* is concerned with is the question of immortality. In the movie, Jesus' sexuality is used to flesh out the implications of mortality if he denies his godhead on the Cross and dies in bed. Jesus (and through him the viewer) is given the ancient Achilleian choice of either living a short life with mythological immortality or living a long, happy life which ends in an obscure and obscuring death. The film (and through it Scorsese is saying Jesus) chooses immortality.

But neither the Bible itself nor the film's fictionalization of Jesus' sexuality probably made much difference to Christians who denounced *The Last Temptation*.[9] Few Christians know very much about the Bible (rarely if ever actually reading any of it but select passages), and no one but a few professionals read biblical scholarship. But most importantly, even fewer have seen the film. What moves them? Is it just intolerance of fantasies that question "truths"? Or, to put the subject in an archetypal perspective, is it a certain kind of fantasy, a spirit or a God that seizes them?

In not seeing the movie, not reading Kazantzakis's novel, not knowing about the libertine tradition in Christianity, Christians are not bound by any rules of empiricism in attacking *The Last Temptation*. Instead they are gripped by what "they do not know." When one is in the state of not knowing something, but feels or acts as if one did, an archetypal situation is making itself manifest. I would like to argue that this "not knowing" is itself a God with a long tradition behind it, the Agnostos Theos, the Deus Ignotus, the Unknown God.

Of particular interest here is the fact that the Unknown God was invented at the same time as Christianity and by the same person who invented Christianity as a religion—Paul. In Acts, Paul goes to Athens after he was thrown out of Thessalonica by the local Jews who objected to his preaching. While in Athens ". . . his spirit was stirred in him, when he saw the city wholly given to idolatry" (Acts 17:16). He argues against "idolatry" with Jewish Athenians, "devout persons," and anyone else he meets in the marketplace. Paul creates such a sensation or disturbance in Athens that "Then certain philosophers of the Epicureans, and of the Stoicks [*sic*], encountered him. And some said, 'What will this babbler say?' other some, 'He seemeth to be a setter forth of strange gods': because he preached unto them Jesus, and the resurrection" (Acts 17:18). The philosophers take him to the Areopagus to ask him what he is talking about and what it means. After a pause for a gratuitous criticism of the Athenian Platonic Academy and its thinkers—"For all the Athenians and strangers which were there spent their time in nothing else, but either to tell, or to hear some new thing"—(Acts 17:21) the narrative resumes: "Then Paul stood in the midst of Mars' hill, and said, 'Ye men of Athens, I perceive that in all things ye are too superstitious. For as I passed by, and beheld your devotions, I found an altar with this inscription, TO THE UNKNOWN GOD. Whom therefore ye ignorantly worship, him declare I unto you'" (Acts 17:22–23).

This altar to the Unknown God is Paul's fiction. The Greeks did not conceive of a singular divinity called the Agnostos Theos, or the Unknown God, but always a multiplicity of "Unknown Gods." The dedication of these altars was always in the ablative plural, "agnostois theois."[10]

Scholars are uncertain of the beliefs and rites surrounding

these altars. One theory is that the altars were set up at different religious sites in order not to offend any local deities that might have become displaced by the introduction of Gods from the East after Alexander's conquests, or to remember Gods that might have become forgotten with time. In this way the altars are imagined as having acted as prophylactics against malevolent influences of slighted local divinities, protection against the wrath of Gods whose names were unknown.

But another theory argues that there is ambiguity as to whether the term meant "to the Unknown Gods" or "to the Unknowable Gods." If they were dedicated to the "Unknowable Gods," their existence would point to a proto-gnostic idea of Gods. Their function would have been to give this theological sensibility a specific space for worship in some Greek temples.

Driven by his own anonymously repressive sexual imagination, Paul cleverly appropriated this ambiguity of the "agnostois theois" altars for his arguments with the Athenian "Epicureans and Stoicks [*sic*]." With his monotheistic vision he did away with the polytheism inherent in the plurality of "Unknown Gods." He deliberately created instead the singular "agnostos theos" which immediately attached itself to the image of Jesus. For the Unknown God (the God of Unknowing, the unconscious side of Christianity), together with the known side, Jesus, easily came to make up an important syzygy in the archetypal religious fantasy of Christianity. The result of Paul's invention has been that Christianity must always carry an intolerance born out of its God of not knowing, its unconscious side, when this God is invoked.

And when is the Unknown God in the Christian syzygy invoked? Clearly in the case of Scorsese's movie. He became vibrantly alive, outraged by what he saw as slurs on his celibacy, fuming at the least suggestion that his humanity bore any trace of a sexual nature, and furious to the point of using arson and terrorism at the very thought of his purity being defiled. In today's Christianity, the Unknown God is far more powerful than the known one.

---

1.   Many of Jesus' early followers took him for a "libertine." This led to a version of Christianity in the early church which sacralized and ritualized the

indulgence in sensual pleasures. This form of Christianity rivaled ascetic Christianity in the first centuries of the religion (but was finally defeated by it). Ascetic Christianity is merely the approved version of the cult practiced today. See Morton Smith, *The Secret Gospel* (New York: Harper & Row, 1973), 75, 112.

2. Michael Baigent, Richard Leigh, and Henry Lincoln, *Holy Blood, Holy Grail* (New York: Delacorte, 1982), 309, and Smith, *The Secret Gospel*, 114.

3. Smith, 70. This Salome is only mentioned once in the Gospel of Mark, but she seems to have been deleted from the other Gospels. Smith specifically shows how she was cut out from an earlier version of Mark at 10:46. She is not to be confused, of course, with the Herodian Salome.

4. *Holy Blood, Holy Grail*, 304–10.

5. Ibid., 310–16, and see John 13:23, 13:25.

6. Smith, at an Eranos lecture in Ascona, Switzerland, in the summer of 1983, presented his ideas on what the secret teachings probably were, particularly what kind of magical rites they might have been and a possible reference to them in 1 John 5:6.

7. Ancient writers suggested that the young man of the story was John. Francis Wright Beare, *The Earliest Records of Jesus* (New York: Abingdon Press, 1962), 230–31.

8. "Through seventeen hundred years of *New Testament* scholarship, nobody has ever been able to explain what that young man was doing alone with Jesus in such a place, at such a time, and in such a costume. All too serious scholars have been reduced to suggesting that the youth was an innocent bystander, walking in his sleep. The business in hand was a baptism; the youth wore the required costume" (Smith, 81).

9. To give an example of the hysterical reaction of some Christians, the producer of the Catholic Cable Television channel, Mother Angelica, proclaimed on her show that *The Last Temptation* was a "holocaustal film as it kills unborn souls in the body of Christ." It is understandable that "a bride of Christ" could not bear seeing the image of her "husband" having sex on a large screen. (Mother Angelica—like most of the film's detractors—had not actually seen the movie.) But to abuse a term like "holocaust" in this context, a word that ought to be reserved forever as referring to history's worst enormity and nothing else, shows how deranged some people got in their own fantasies of this movie.

10. The phrase "agnoston theon" was found on two altars observed by Pausanias in his *Periegesis*, one at Olympia and the other at Phaleron. See *The Encyclopedia of Religion*, ed. Mircea Eliade, vol. 1 (New York: Macmillan, 1987), 135.

THE LAST SOCIAL FUNCTION OF CHRIST

MORTON SMITH

The protests and picketing evoked by Scorsese's film *The Last Temptation of Christ* bring to attention again a long-standing problem of psychohistory: What is the importance of Christ in contemporary American religion?

The problem is so difficult because there are so many answers. To begin with the most obvious, "Christ" is a fundamental element of the theological structure and governmental theory of all Christian denominations. The Pope claims to be his representative ("vicar") on earth, and persons or groups in most Christian bodies make substantially similar claims in more or less disguised forms. Compare the Lord Chancellor's song in *Iolanthe*:

> The Law is the true embodiment
> Of everything that's excellent;
> It has no kind of fault or flaw.
> And I, my Lords, embody the law.

What "the Law" is to legal theory and the legal establishment, Christ is to Christian theology and the Christian establishment.

Since the Christian establishment in the United States (according to the latest *World Almanac*) claims about 79 million Protestants, 53 million Roman Catholics, and 7 millions of other denominations—in all, 159 millions, of whom possibly half are children, leaving about 80 million adults of whom possibly half take Christian teachings seriously—anything that both tends to discredit Christ and seems likely to attract much attention is pretty sure to run into trouble. Though practicing Christians make up about a sixth of the population (roughly 40 of 250 millions), they practice in a society that officially approves and legally favors them, and they can always get attention, usually favorable, by the media, by legislators, and by officials on all levels from the police to the President.

However, among the two-thirds of the population who are not practicing Christians, there are lots to be attracted by a naturalistic, or even unfavorable, treatment of Jesus (the human element in the Christ figure). And there are lots more who will go to see a picture known as "controversial" so as to "keep up" with the controversy. ("Keeping up" with current topics is one of the things that makes Mrs. Sammy run, not walk, and so contributes to Sammy's chronic indigestion.)

Consequently, it would be interesting to know how much it cost the advertising agency handling *The Last Temptation* to make sure that the film would be adequately protested and picketed, and that these events would get proper attention.

Whatever the means, the film is now "controversial" and—I understand—doing nicely. Because of the attention attracted, its owners will probably not be able to get it shown in many small places with solidly or belligerently Christian populations whom the owners of the local picture houses cannot afford to antagonize. But the big cities, where the houses can disregard (and may even welcome) picketing, can furnish a big income.

A test case was the last previously "irreverent" life of Jesus, Monty Python's *Life of Brian*. I believe "Brian" had to be substituted for "Jesus" to enable the picture to be shown in England (that citadel of liberalism). Nevertheless, the reference was unmistakable and the picketing was readily secured, the more so because, since the picture pretended not to refer to Jesus, it could display the sexual attractions and sardonic humor for which Python films are famous. When the crucified Brian and his crucified companions swung into "Look on the Sunny Side of Life," the artistic increment was inversely proportional to the decline of the expectable audience. For a history of religion in the United States, it would be interesting to have a list of the places in which *Brian* was shown and the amounts it grossed in each.

A similar list for *Last Temptation* would be even more interesting, since it deals explicitly with *Jesus* (no pseudonym), but does so on the level of high drama, and limits its sexual shots to his daydreams during the tedium of crucifixion. "Reverence for humanity and for human needs and hopes" (in mostly tacit contrast to Jesus' traditional career and goals) is the implicit theme of the work, and this is also the theme of the powerful and popular side of American religion. Where *Brian* appealed almost exclusively to the anti- or non-Christian population, *The Last Temptation* evidently hopes to reach also the great body of liberal Christians and sympathetic non-Christians, all of whom have made their religious concern the living of a good life in this world. How far will it succeed?

The answer to that question will depend on an incalculable number of incalculable variants, many of them the quirks and powers of individuals who set fashions in various communities. Advertising will try to deal with this variety by inventing praises of general appeal, and hostile propaganda by producing similar attacks. But both will have to consider the question from which we started: What is the importance of Christ in American religion? We have spoken of his theological and organizational roles, but what is he in the lives of the Christians?

So many things: the good shepherd in beautifully laundered linen, with a snow-white lamb cradled in his arm; the bambino, himself cradled in the Madonna's arms or sitting up, haloed, to bless those presenting their requests at her shrine; the center of the festivals of Christmas and Easter; the awful judge of the last judgment, in some stained glass window copied from a Gothic original; the body around the Sacred Heart; the hero of the four gospels (or, at least, of those portions generally read); the mysterious presence in the Sacrament of the Altar; "Jesus, lover of my soul" in the old ladies' and young acolytes' favorite hymn (to waltz time); the Word of God, only-begotten Son of the Father, and Second Person of the Blessed Trinity; the central figure of innumerable crucifixions, from the flowery Perugino to the stark Rouault—the historical definition could go on indefinitely. But how did a Galilean peasant boy happen to become all these things?

The historical attempts to answer this question are minimal elements in the meaning of Jesus to modern American Christians. In the nineteenth century, when the bourgeoisie still believed in history, would-be historical lives of Jesus had more importance for popular thought than may be expected for *The Last Temptation*. Now, there have been too many "historical" Jesuses. Consequently, there are few subjects of Christian literature about which the average literate Christian thinks less.

Nevertheless, the question "How did the peasant boy become the Christ" must have not only a historical, but also a general psychological answer: he became an idea.

The idea is already there in the Gospel according to John 10:30: "The Father and I are one." As has often been recognized, this broke the antithesis between the sole, invisible, omnipotent, eternal God, in whom the thought of the critical theologians of the Old Testament—above all "second Isaiah" (Is. 40–55)—had culminated, and the pagan recognition of deity in nature and especially in men and the works of men. In spite of the poetry of the second Isaiah and the author of Job, the God of Old Testament rationalism (as distinct from other strains in the Old Testament) remains apart, almost impersonal, less predictable than a cosmic force, but little more amiable. In Job, as a matter of fact, he almost becomes the Enemy; Job is the precursor of the "gnostic" theologies in which the creator of this world and of natural law is the power of evil. Similarly impersonal, inflexible, and therefore potentially inimical were the gods of pagan philosophy; they were occasionally praised, but very rarely worshiped. The worship of the Greco-Roman world went to gods of human form and personality with whom men could be joined by interest and affection and sometimes even united physically, gods who had sons like Jesus, "the Son of God," the God who had gone about Galilee doing miracles, had suffered and died and risen and gone up to heaven. Between such gods and the "Cosmocrators"—the world rulers—there was a world of difference.

When the author of John made Jesus say, "The Father and I are one," those two concepts of Godhead were fused. The new God was both the Father—cosmic, austere law, the ideal to be obeyed—and the Son—human, capable of love and death, of suffering and, therefore, of sympathy and forgiveness.

Hence the incredibly multifarious picture (reviewed above) of Jesus-Christ, the man-God, and hence, too, his social function, to reconcile those united with him to the world of law and order and physical necessity which must be served, even to death. Hence, too, the instinctive resistance of Christians to the historical study of Jesus and to any presentation of him in a naturalistic novel in which he would live a fully human life. For his function as mediator he must remain united with the Father. His union, as Son, with the Father and his union, as God, with his humanity are by nature inscrutable mysteries of the faith.

If these holy mysteries of theology sound very much like the holy mysteries of psychology, if the Father and the superego have a surprising family resemblance (and so on down), that may explain why so many millions have found in this theological structure a framework for the structuring of their own personalities and have also found in the gospel stories models for solutions of particular personal problems. Hence, further, it is understandable that a film which threatens to break down the theological structure—even if only indirectly, by suggestion—will arouse, from Christians quite ignorant of theology, reactions more violent than the film's rather commonplace content would lead us to expect. To put the matter in a nutshell, for many Christians Jesus is Christ, Christ is God, and this God is the invisible framework of their lives.

THE "STONE"
WHICH IS NOT A STONE
C. G. Jung and the Postmodern
Meaning of "Meaning"

DAVID L. MILLER

Depth psychology—along with post-Einsteinian physics, post-Saussurean structuralist linguistics, and post-Heideggerian philosophy[1]—is a contributor to the revolution in the meaning of "meaning" in the twentieth century. Concerning this revolution, it is surely not sufficient to say, as has Thomas Kuhn, that the paradigm of meaning has shifted.[2] The transformations indicated by these disciplines are so radical as to have made the paradigm of "paradigm" itself not pertinent, belonging as it does to a meaning of "meaning" which implies an Aristotelian principle of identity. Terms like "charm" in physics and *glissement* in semiotics indicate a fundamentally different principle working in their logics, a principle of difference which, as Bachelard argued, is radically non-Aristotelian.[3]

It has been shown by Jacques Lacan, Julia Kristeva and Norman O. Brown (among others) that Freud's discoveries and his discourse share in and promote the decentering Copernican revolution in thought, even against Freud's intention and his reductive rhetoric. Although he was hampered by his own use of a causal mechanistic logic and a habituated scientistic notion of "meaning," Freud's texts, nonetheless, reveal the revolutionary nature of his own thinking about thinking. The same is true of Jung. The latter is fully participant in a radical moment in what C. K. Ogden and I. A. Richards have called "the meaning of meaning,"[4] and though the diction of Jung's language masks revolutionary implications in his thinking, they are there boldly in his texts all the same. Little attempt (apart from the work of Paul Kugler and Ed Casey) has been made to show this side of Jung's writings, which is why some demonstration, such as the following, may be needed.

That Jung was himself interested in the question of the meaning of "meaning" has been established firmly, were it not already obvious, by Aniela Jaffé in her book *The Myth of Meaning in the Work of C. G. Jung.*[5] However, Jaffé seems to locate Jung's sense of so-called "meaning" in a "unitary"[6] paradigm, thereby obscuring its radical nature. She notes that Jung identified a sense of meaninglessness with psychoneurosis,[7] and she reports that Jung "cherished the anxious hope that meaning will preponderate" over meaninglessness.[8] Sentiments such as these are clearly ruled more by an Aristotelian principle of identity than they are by a postmodern perspective of difference. Yet, already in Jaffé's title, where "meaning" is spoken of (as it is in the book itself) as a "myth," there is a chink in the armor of protective Aristotelianism. Indeed, Jaffé notes that for Jung the "myth of meaning is the myth of consciousness,"[9] which on Jung's own terms makes "meaning" one-sided or neurotic. Furthermore, Jaffé names one of her chapters "The Hidden Reality," referring to the fact that the nature of so-called "meaning" is such that it can never be apparent or expressed. Jaffé says that "up to the end of his life Jung allotted a place for both meaning and meaninglessness in his scheme of things."[10] And Jaffé faithfully reports that Jung thought "meaning" was a "conjecture,"[11] and that when, one day late in his life, he was talking in his home to a group of psychiatrists from America, England and Switzerland, after telling them they needed to create a myth of meaning for themselves, Jung added, "then you have to learn to become decently unconscious."[12]

Indeed, though Jung was fond of suspiciously Aristotelian terms, like "identity," "identification," "union," *unio mentalis,* "unifying function," "harmony," and "coincidence," and though Jung often wrote dogmatically that this *is* that, or that such-and-such without equivocation *refers to* "anima" or "shadow" or "self," nonetheless, when he reflected on the nature of his own psychological reflections, from the Zofingia lectures in his student days until the very end of his life, there is always a deferral of certainty in identifications and an affirmation of doubleness and difference in the interest of realistic self-knowledge and therapeutic generosity. Nowhere is this radical edge to Jung's critical thinking plainer than in his use of the phrase "nothing but" (*nichts als*).

Jung borrowed this phrase, which he used so often, from William James, as he himself tells us.[13] James had written, in his book on *Pragmatism*, that when "what is higher is explained by what is lower and treated forever as a case of 'nothing but,' " the reasoning is faulty.[14] Jung extended James's use of the phrase "nothing but" to include thinking about something whose nature is unknowable as if it could be known and, more simply, thinking or speaking about something in a one-sided or definite manner when a humble reticence or generous agnosticism would have been more appropriate.[15]

Jung admitted that the world likes its "meaning" ruled by the principle of identity which makes notions of "nothing but" possible. He said: "Patients and doctors alike want to hear that neurosis is a 'nothing but.' "[16] However, against the grain of the people and the profession, Jung was strongly—even passionately—opposed to such thinking about his own thinking in such a way. He called "nothing but" thinking by names such as "repressive,"[17] "not healthy,"[18] "neurotic,"[19] "one-sided,"[20] "soulless,"[21] "banal,"[22] "Mephistophelean,"[23] "obsessive,"[24] "infantile,"[25] "hysterical,"[26] "destructive,"[27] "sterile,"[28] "reductionist,"[29] and "cheap."[30] Jung's language is strong, and it speaks against Jungians, as much as Freudians, when the former fall into the habit of saying, "this is an anima-problem" or "that is a father–daughter complex," believing thereby that one has said something. No wonder Jung said, "Thank God I am ... not a Jungian" and even went so far as to say, "I can only hope and wish that no one becomes 'Jungian.' "[31] Indeed, in the case of

Freud, Jung noted that "nothing but" thinking is often, as he put it, "the fate of second generation" followers of great thinkers.[32] Jung explicitly linked "certainty," in the Cartesian sense, with "nothing but" thinking,[33] and he warned that such fantasies about one's knowledge and understanding were protective, defensive mechanisms against the perceived threat of the unknown.[34]

Jung, for his part, was "clear" about not being clear. In speaking about "nothing but" thinking, he remarked: "I trust I have given no cause for the misunderstanding that I know anything about the nature of the 'centre' [of the Self]—for it is simply unknowable.... "[35] Again, Jung wrote: "We all have far too much the standpoint of the nothing-but psychology, that is, we still think that the new future which is pressing in at the door can be squeezed into the framework of what is already known."[36] In a letter, he reminded one woman that "you cannot possibly learn analytical psychology by studying its object, since it consists exclusively of what you don't know about yourself."[37] When Heinrich Zimmer dedicated a book to Jung with the words "master of those who know," Jung wrote Zimmer, chiding him by saying that "your gladdening dedication ... , however, keeps it a secret that everything I know comes from my mastery of not-knowing."[38] Jung corrected another admirer by mail, saying, "the concept of the unconscious *posits nothing*, it designates only my *unknowing*."[39] In his memoirs, Jung said that by utilizing the term "unconscious," depth psychological discourse is "admitting that it knows nothing about it, for it can know nothing about the substance of the psyche when the sole means of knowing anything is the psyche."[40] And in "Answer to Job," Jung wrote "I am conscious that I am moving in a world of images and that none of my reflections touches the essence of the unknowable."[41] It is in keeping with this deference based upon the principle of difference that Jung says, at the end of his memoirs, that he concurs with Lao Tzu. "All are clear, I alone am clouded."[42] This is to say: all are with Descartes and Aristotle, but "meaning" for me has a different meaning.

In 1906, Jung wrote in support of Aristotle's "laws of association ... simultaneity ... [and] similarity."[43] That was the period in which Jung was working on word-association tests. But as his life and work went on, his view against Aristotle became as adamant as his view against the adamantine nature of "nothing but" thinking. Already in 1934 he warned against those persons who had reticence about overthrowing prior philosophical assumptions,[44] and at Eranos in 1938 he argued that an "Aristotelian reasoning" produces a "nominalism" in thinking that works against depth psychology, generally, and against the concept of archetype, particularly.[45] As Jung moved into his later interest in the logic of alchemy as an analogue for the logic of depth psychology, his statements against Aristotelian principles of reasoning became even stronger. He cites the alchemist Dorn, who said: "Whoever wishes to learn the alchemical art, let him learn not the philosophy of Aristotle, but that which teaches the truth . . . for his teaching . . . is the best of all cloaks for lies."[46] And Jung cites with approval the plea of Padrizi to Pope Gregory XIV to allow Hermes to replace Aristotle as the philosopher of the Church![47]

In his memoirs, Jung says that early in his career he "had not yet found the right language" for his work, but that with alchemy he discovered "a mythopoeic imagination," as opposed to a "nothing but" thinking.[48] Jung says: ". . . I realized the concordance between this poetic myth [the Grail legend] and what alchemy had to say about the *unum vas*, the *una medicina*, and the *unus lapis*."[49] Thus, Jung came to a poetic, mythic, symbolic and metaphoric understanding of the meaning of "meaning" in his own psychological discourse. Unity could never more be conceived of under the Aristotelian principle of identity. The way in which Jung handled the concept of the *unus lapis*, "the one [philosopher's] stone," shows Jung's thinking ruled by the principle, not of identity, but of difference, since, concerning the idea of the *lapis philosophorum*, Jung says directly that one cannot make meaningful sense out of it with reasoning of the "nothing but" sort.[50]

The "philosopher's stone," Jung says, was the goal of the alchemical *opus*,[51] and, by analogy, it was the goal of therapy (i.e., individuation) as well. Jung liked to quote the alchemist's injunction "Transform yourselves into living philosophical stones!"[52] But what does this mean? What is this stone?

It is many things, to be sure,[53] and yet it is one.[54] Indeed, it is both the one and the many,[55] and at the same time mediator between one and many.[56] It is a bird,[57] and it is food.[58] It is body and flesh,[59] and it is spirit and life.[60] It is pain,[61] and, in the form of Christ, it is salvation from pain.[62] Above all, it is a stone (common and rejected by people as unimportant),[63] and yet it is not a stone. Jung often cited the formula *"lithos ou lithos,"* "the stone which is not a stone."[64] It is surely plain that no meaning of "meaning" which is based on a principle of identity is implied in any of this.

Indeed, though the "stone" has speech, or is language,[65] its discourse, according to Jung, is that of image and metaphor.[66] All knowledge of the "stone" and by way of the "stone" is metaphoric or, as Jung liked to say, symbolic. Jung stressed this again and again.[67]

If alchemy, in Jung's own view, is the clue to the nature of the logic of his psychological discourse, if the *lapis philosophorum* is the "treasure" of that discourse which itself speaks, and if turning to the logic of alchemy for a depth psyche-logic means a turning away from Aristotle and from thinking of the "nothing but" type, then a radical transformation of the meaning of so-called "meaning" is implied in the mature texts of C. G. Jung.

It is hardly surprising that the symbology of the stone should have been a clue to Jung's radical sense of the meaning of "meaning." He tells how in his childhood he used to sit on a particular stone in front of the wall in the yard when he was troubled with questions of "meaning." While sitting on the stone, his perplexity would be displaced to a new conundrum. In Jung's words, "the question then arose: 'Am I the one sitting on the stone, or am I the stone on which *he* is sitting?' "[68] Even in midlife, Jung would go back to that stone and sit on it, wondering "whether it was I or I was it."[69] Jung reports that whenever he thought about the "secret significance" of the stone, the conflict between meaning and meaninglessness ceased.[70] The stone, Jung said, was "the Other in me."[71] It is surely this other Jung, speaking "as a poet," as Russell Lockhart has so well explained,[72] who said: "Life at the core is steel on stone."[73]

Concerning the "coveted substance, the *lapis*," the unity represented by it as the goal is, as Jung says, "not really a question of identification at all." Aristotle's principle of identity does not apply. Rather, as Jung says, it is really a matter of "the hermeneutic *sicut*—'as' or 'like.'"[74] And the hermeneutic or poetic "as" implies difference. The so-called "stone" is not a stone; it "is" a bird, food, Christ, one, many, etc. And the "is" in this sentence is functioning like an "as."[75] By this strategy, Jung notes, "the alchemist . . . stresses . . . humility."[76]

So, Jung would come to say that the self, which is like the "stone" which is not a stone, is of such a nature that psychological discourse "would rather not speak of it."[77] In this sentiment, Jung was repeating a comment on the *lapis* made at Eranos in 1935 by Rudolf Bernoulli. The latter said: "No words or images are adequate for the communication of this . . . and the few who have known of them have found but one means of expression: silence."[78] It goes without saying that this perspective corresponds to Jung's view of the function of the concept of the "unconscious" in depth psychology.

It corresponds also with Jung's notion of what he called "the archetype of meaning." This psychological complex was represented, for Jung, by figures such as the Old Wise Woman and the Wise Old Man. But since these figures always presented themselves with two sides—that is, with simultaneous difference —the meaning of the "meaning" conveyed in such imaginal figures had constantly to be deferred, rendering the psychologist—like the alchemist—agnostic, ironic, and humble.[79] Jung, like Heidegger, came to see that if "meaning" of an Aristotelian sort is too much insisted upon, it is only a matter of time until that very "meaning" will, by what Jung called a "bold enantiodromia,"[80] turn into its opposite. Meaninglessness is built into the very archetype of meaning. The course of wisdom consists in deferring one-sided judgment concerning meaning.

This deferral in the interest of individuated difference is just what Jacques Derrida's neologism *différance* means to suggest.

It means to stress both ontological "difference," as did Kierke-
gaard and Heidegger, and it means further to suggest human
"deferral" forever of identifications with and attachments to
pretensions of truth and claims to "meaning," all in the interest
of deference for life and health, not to mention good manners.[81]

The idea in this shift from identity to difference is to live
among "integers of difference [in life] that set up no resonance of
relation"[82] without requiring of oneself or of one's object an
agreement or identification. The mood of differentiating (or individuating as Jung called it), rather than identifying, consists in
letting things be, allowing worlds to presence themselves,
bracketing the question of "meaning" or "meaninglessness" in
the mode of those Oriental philosophies which stress "such-
ness."[83] The obsession with certainty, with truth and so-called
"meaning" would give way to living in the wondrous world of
multiplicity, being with such worlds as they are, in a mode of
generosity and humility with regard to truth and "meanings."

Jung's way of expressing this pre-Derridean *différance* was by
using the term "symbolic." "Every view," he once wrote,
"which interprets the symbolic expression as an analogue of an
abbreviated designation for a known thing is *semiotic*. A view
which interprets the symbolic expression as the best possible
formulation of a relatively unknown thing, which for that
reason cannot be more clearly or characteristically expressed, is
symbolic."[84] This is the well-known distinction between signs
and symbols which occurs in Jungian, Tillichian and other post-
Kantian orthodoxies of the early twentieth century. Signs point
to something known; symbols participate in that to which they
point and involve depth, mystery, and the unknown. They are
the mode appropriate to epistemological humility.

But James Hillman, among others, has pointed out that as time
has gone by symbolism has veered away from the unknown in
the direction of the known. In Jungian psychological ortho-
praxy we know that cats in men's dreams "mean" *anima*, that
eggs in women's dreams "mean" fecundity, and so on.[85] Aristotle
and his principle of identity are reborn, and Jung and the depth
in his psychology are lost. There is an irony in this.

In post-Saussurean linguistics, semiology indicates the radically gappy or paratactic nature of so-called "meaning" in which the principle of difference is honored. Symbolism now indicates the presence of residual semantic security based in Aristotle's principle of identity.[86] If Jung were today to make his point about psychological discourse implying an "unknowing," he would have to call it "semiotic" in order to protect the radicalness of the nature of his meaning from the fate of the second generation who deal with symbols, not symbolically, but as significations of knowledge.

It is, then, no surprise that Jung, in good postmodern fashion, when he was fifty-four, wrote: "Life is crazy and meaningful at once. And when we do not laugh over the one aspect and speculate about the other, life is exceedingly drab, and everything is reduced to the littlest scale. There is then little sense and little nonsense either. When you come to think about it, nothing has any meaning, for when there was nobody to think, there was nobody to interpret what happened. Interpretations are only for those who don't understand. . . . "[87] Twenty-nine years later, when he was eighty-four, Jung added: "Which element we think outweighs the other, whether meaninglessness or meaning, is a matter of temperament. . . . Probably, as in all metaphysical questions, both are true: Life is—or has—meaning and meaninglessness."[88] So-called "meaning" is forever deferred. Psychological difference and differentiation are affirmed. The "stone" is not a stone.

1.   Cf. Jeffrey Hopper, *Understanding Modern Theology*, I (Philadelphia: Fortress Press, 1987).

2.   Thomas Kuhn, *The Structure of Scientific Revolutions* (Chicago: University of Chicago Press, 1970).

3.   Gaston Bachelard, *The Philosophy of No*, tr. G. C. Waterson (New York: Orion, 1966).

4.   C. K. Ogden and I. A. Richards, *The Meaning of Meaning* (New York: Harcourt Brace, 1956).

5.   Aniela Jaffé, *The Myth of Meaning*, tr. R. F. C. Hull (New York: Putnam's Sons, 1971).

6.   Ibid., 153; cf. C. G. Jung, *Collected Works* [hereafter *CW*], 9, ii, §264 [indicating volume and paragraph numbers]; and, Maude Oakes, *The Stone Speaks: The Memoir of a Personal Transformation* (Wilmette: Chiron Publications, 1987), 131f.

7. Jung, *CW* 11, §497; Jung, *Memories, Dreams, Reflections* (New York: Vintage Books, 1965), 340; cf. Jaffé, 146.

8. Jung, *Memories, Dreams, Reflections*, 358f.; cf. Jaffé, *Myth of Meaning*, 11.

9. Jung, *Memories, Dreams, Reflections*, 140.

10. Ibid., 146.

11. Ibid., 141.

12. Ibid., 149.

13. Jung, *CW* 3, §423; cf. *CW* 12, §11n., *CW* 16, §98n.

14. Cited in Jung, *CW* 12, §11n.

15. For example, Jung, *CW* 11, §§379, 800, 857; *CW* 17, §302.

16. Jung, *CW* 10, §365.

17. Jung, *CW* 7, §400.

18. Jung, *CW* 8, §711.

19. Jung, *CW* 10, §362.

20. Ibid., §658.

21. Ibid., §357.

22. Jung, *CW* 18, §627.

23. Jung, *CW* 6, §§315, 593.

24. Ibid., §600.

25. Ibid.

26. Ibid.

27. Ibid., §593.

28. Ibid.

29. Jung, *CW* 3, §423, etc.

30. Jung, *CW* 6, §593.

31. Cited in James Yandell, *The Imitation of Jung* (St. Louis: Centerpoint, 1977), 30f.

32. Jung, *CW* 10, §658.

33. Ibid., §35.

34. Jung, *CW* 18, §633.

35. Jung, *CW* 12, §327; cf. D. Miller, "An Other Jung and an Other," *C. G. Jung and the Humanities* (Princeton: Princeton University Press, forthcoming).

36. Jung, *CW* 4, §668.

37. Jung, *Letters*, ed. G. Adler, tr. R. F. C. Hull (Princeton: Princeton University Press, 1975), vol. 1, 90.

38. Ibid., 250.

39. Ibid., 411.

40. Jung, *Memories, Dreams, Reflections*, 336.

41. Jung, *CW* 11, §556.

42. Jung, *Memories, Dreams, Reflections*, 359.

43. Jung, *CW* 2, §268.

44. Jung, *CW* 8, §655.

45. Jung, *CW* 9, i, §149.

46. Cited in Jung, *CW* 14, §425n.

47. Jung, *CW* 12, §478.

48. Jung, *Memories, Dreams, Reflections*, 188.

49. Ibid., 282.

50. Jung, *CW* 12, § 160.

51. Jung, *CW* 13, §§ 245, 425.

52. Jung, *CW* 9, ii, § 264; *CW* 11, § 154; *CW* 12, §§ 187, 378; *CW* 13, § 286.

53. Jung, *CW* 9, ii, § 387; *CW* 11, §§ 707, 807; *CW* 13, §§ 125, 180.

54. Jung, *CW* 14, § 772.

55. Jung, *CW* 9, ii, § 264; *CW* 14, § 496.

56. Jung, *CW* 13, § 131; *CW* 14, § 765.

57. Jung, *CW* 13, § 321; *CW* 14, § 245.

58. Jung, *CW* 14, § 525.

59. Jung, *CW* 9, i, § 555; *CW* 9, ii, § 387; *CW* 12, § 378; *CW* 13, §§ 127, 128, 132, 133; *CW* 14, § 643.

60. Jung, *CW* 9, i, § 246; *CW* 11, § 151; *CW* 12, § 405; *CW* 13, §§ 132, 380f., 390; *CW* 14, § 643.

61. Jung, *CW* 13, § 94.

62. Jung, *CW* 9, ii, § 122; *CW* 13, §§ 127, 132, 162; *CW* 14, § 525n.403.

63. Jung, *CW* 9, i, §§ 248n.18, 165n.59; *CW* 12, §§ 103, 246n.125, 390; *CW* 13, §§ 182n.61, 426, 429.

64. Jung, *CW* 9, i, § 555; *CW* 11, § 707; *CW* 13, § 381n.9; *CW* 14, §§ 626, 643.

65. Jung, *CW* 9, i, § 238; cf. Jung, *Memories, Dreams, Reflections*, 227; and Oakes, *The Stone Speaks*, 131 and passim.

66. Jung, *CW* 9, ii, § 213f.; *CW* 14, § 627.

67. Jung, *CW* 11, § 153; *CW* 12, §§ 451, 564; *CW* 13, §§ 131, 431; *CW* 14, §§ 212f.; *CW* 16, §§ 414n.7, 498.

68. Jung, *Memories, Dreams, Reflections*, 20.

69. Ibid. There is also the important personal association of Jung's between the *lapis philosophorum* and his "stone" at Bollingen. See Oakes, *The Stone Speaks*, passim. Oakes's interpretation and the present one are fundamentally different. Concerning the stone, Jung said to Oakes, as she herself reports: "The stone is nothing. I am not an artist; I did it to amuse myself. It is a holiday thing—as if I sang a stone" (ibid., 15). And about her manuscript, Jung said: "I find it a bit too intellectual" (ibid., 24), though he had also said that what he had to say "cannot be shown to those who do not think" (ibid., 15). It is the perspective of the present argument that the intellectualism resides in the Aristotelian principle of identity which will always ask, as Oakes does, for "an inner meaning" (ibid., 28) and will answer the question of meaning with statements like "the stone is Hermes" or "it symbolizes a river" (ibid., 91 and passim). If it *is* this or that, it cannot also be some other. Aristotle's principle of A = A and not not-A is engaged (against Jung). But if the stone *is* not this and not that, if it *is* nothing, no-thing, not some-thing, then it can be taken *as* this and that, all of which may be different from it. If, for example, it *is* not wholeness, then it can be whole, that is, it can be all things, everything that it is not. The "stone" then *is* not a stone. This means that the stone speaks precisely when it is silent. When it speaks, it does not. A *stone* speaks precisely because it does not speak. Jung's stone "spoke" because the scratchings on the stone did not lead to knowledge; otherwise, on Jung's own terms, we could not call them symbols. But since they do lead to intellectual knowledge in

Oakes's reading, we now must call them signs, rather than symbols, to protect the psyche, the un-conscious, and the un-knowing.

70. Jung, *Memories, Dreams, Reflections*, 42.

71. Ibid.

72. Russell Lockhart, *Psyche Speaks: A Jungian Approach to Self and World* (Wilmette: Chiron Publications, 1987), 24–26, 73–79, esp. 74–75, where the author makes a point similar to the one being made in this section, albeit in a different way.

73. Jung, *Letters*, vol. 2, 119.

74. Jung, *CW* 12, § 451.

75. See Stanley Hopper, "The Bucket as It Is," in *Metaphor and Beyond* (Syracuse: Alteracts, 1979), where the author offers the following formula: "When as is as as, then as is as is."

76. Jung, *CW* 12, § 451.

77. Ibid., 313.

78. Rudolf Bernoulli, "Spiritual Development in Alchemy," in *Spiritual Disciplines: Papers from the Eranos Yearbooks*, ed. J. Campbell (New York: Pantheon, 1960), 320. Cf. Oakes, *The Stone Speaks*, 15, where the author recalls a conversation with Jung: "The Stone is nothing. . . . I don't know who I am. I'm the last person to tell you who I am. I'm invisible. I am nothing; I am an old man. I no longer lie. Once, perhaps, I had to, as a young scientist without a reputation. Now I no longer lie. What I have to say is so simple that it is hard to understand. . . . It cannot be shown to those who do not think."

79. Jung, *CW* 9, i, §§ 67–72, 682, esp. 413.

80. Ibid., § 417.

81. Jacques Derrida, *Of Grammatology*, tr. G. C. Spivak (Baltimore: Johns Hopkins University Press, 1974), lix: "At the point where the concept of *différance* intervenes . . . all the conceptual oppositions of metaphysics [like meaning and meaninglessness] . . . become non-pertinent." Cf. ibid., xxix, xliii, 143; and Derrida, *Dissemination*, tr. B. Johnson (Chicago: University of Chicago Press, 1981), viii–x; Derrida, *Writing and Difference*, tr. A. Bass (Chicago: University of Chicago Press, 1978), 198; and Derrida, "La différance," *Bulletin de la société française de philosophie* 62/3 (1968). Also, see Carl Raschke, "The Deconstruction of God," in T. J. J. Altizer et al., *Deconstruction and Theology* (New York: Crossroads, 1982), 8–11: "*différance* . . . is the continuous production of significance through displacement" (10).

82. Stanley R. Hopper, " 'Le Cri de Merlin!' On Interpretation and the Metalogical," in *Anagogic Qualities of Literature*, ed. J. Strelka (University Park: Pennsylvania State University Press, 1971), 26.

83. See ibid., 23–33; and Hopper, "The Bucket as It Is," 5–47.

84. Jung, *CW* 6, § 815 (italics added).

85. James Hillman, "An Inquiry into Image," *Spring 1977*: 67.

86. See Jean Graybeal, *Language and "the Feminine" in Nietzsche and Heidegger* (Ann Arbor: University Microfilms International, 1986), 18–30; Julia Kristeva, *Desire in Language*, ed. Leon Roudiez (New York: Columbia University Press, 1980), 133f.; Julia Kristeva, "Il n'y a pas de maitre a langage," *Nouvelle revue de psychanalyse* 20 (Autumn 1979): 37, 128ff.; Julia Kristeva,

"The Semiotic and the Symbolic," in *Revolution in Poetic Language*, tr. M. Waller (New York: Columbia University Press, 1984), 28–29; D. Miller, "An Other Jung and an Other," passim.

87. Jung, *CW* 10, §65.

88. Jung, *Memories, Dreams, Reflections*, 358f. Jaffé interprets these sayings of Jung's quite differently. She focuses on the next line, in which Jung says, "but I cherish the anxious hope that meaning will preponderate" (see note 8, above). Unfortunately, for her view, Jung had already blunted her argument and his own anxious "hope" by saying, "It is a matter of temperament," which presumably includes the temperaments of Jung himself, Jaffé, and the present writer. Though Jung's statement indicates his own personal temperament, against Jaffé's reading (which, nonetheless, is a possible one), Jung's statement does not hamper a radical reading of the postmodern edge in his psychology. It only attests to dated diction. However, not all of Jung's diction is out of date. Indeed, some sounds strikingly post-Derridean. Hillman has found eloquent testimony by Jung himself to the logic of "difference." See Hillman, "Jung's Daimonic Inheritance," *Sphinx* 1 (1988): 12. For example: Jung, *CW* 6, §§705, 757; *CW* 11, §855f.; *CW* 13, §§73–75, 395; *CW* 17, §289.

ARCHITECTURE AND THE ANIMA MUNDI
Transformations in Sacred Space

A. VERNON WOODWORTH

> He looked at Gilgamesh and said:
> You will be left alone, unable to understand
> In a world where nothing lives anymore
> As you thought it did. . . .
> That is what it is to be a man. You'll know
> When you have lost the strength to see
> The way you once did.
> You'll be alone and wander
> Looking for that life that's gone or some
> Eternal life you have to find.
> He drew closer to his friend's face.
> My pain is that my eyes and ears
> No longer see and hear the same
> As yours do.
>
> *Gilgamesh*

I. Preface

The timeless epic of Gilgamesh and Enkidu depicts the initial enmity, eventual friendship, and ultimate tragedy of the joining of humanity's animal and divine natures. The tale is a tragedy for Enkidu because his experience of sexual love with a woman has caused him to become aware of his separateness from his animal companions. This leads him into the company of man where he meets, fights, and wins the affection of the god-man Gilgamesh. It is a tragedy for Gilgamesh because the eventual death of his beloved friend forces him to face life's most baffling certainty, sending him on a desperate search which can only end in failure.

This confrontation with mortality is stated explicitly by Enkidu to be the essence of the human condition, and the quest for immortality by Gilgamesh is generally considered to be the dramatic dynamic underlying this epic. Yet a careful reading of Enkidu's deathbed speech reveals another interpretation. It is not so much the finite nature of things, the inevitability of death, which disturbs Enkidu as it is the failure of these things to resonate with vitality as they did in his previous mode of animal consciousness. The knowledge of death—which, like the knowledge of good and evil for Adam and Eve, separates man from his natural surroundings and alienates him from his animal nature—causes him as well to "see death in things" where previously "everything had life to me."

Having lost his connection to the animal consciousness represented by Enkidu, Gilgamesh in grief sets out to discover an antidote to this tragic state of consciousness, a solution to the alienation and lack of meaning caused by a knowledge of death and living in a world of dead things. Although everyone along the way assures him of the futility of his quest, he continues, perhaps haunted by Enkidu's words:

> . . . you'll be alone and wander
> Looking for that life that's gone or some
> Eternal life you have to find.

After finding and then losing to an opportunistic serpent the plant of immortality, Gilgamesh returns defeated to his Babylonian city.

> He looked at the walls,
> Awed at the heights
> His people had achieved
> And for a moment—just a moment—

All that lay behind him
Passed from view.[1]

The sense of loss and longing which adheres to the tragic creation of ego-consciousness has been expressed throughout history in myths, legends and art. Jung, following Levy-Bruhl, referred to this lost state of paradise as "participation mystique," an absence of differentiation between subject and object, or figure and ground. In such a condition, there is no ego to discriminate between internal and external motivations or between subjective "emotion" and objective "matter." No limit is set on the dynamic flow of life, for all creation participates in the vitality of Being.

Coming at this condition from the perspective of a Western "psychological" ego, we are inclined to suspect a basic fallacy, an error of perception based on "unconsciousness" which obscures the irreconcilable opposition between subject and object. This view, while different from fundamental Eastern assumptions of the nature of reality, is foreshadowed in the Gilgamesh epic where the synthesis of our god-like (spiritual) and animal-like (instinctual) natures into human form involves breaking this spell, a fall from Paradise, and the awareness of our aloneness, our finite nature, and the inevitability of death.

Jung says regarding projection:

> Thus every normal person of our time, who is not reflective beyond the average, is bound to his environment by a whole system of projections. So long as all goes well, he is totally unaware of the compulsive, i.e., "magical" or "mystical" character of these relationships. . . . But as soon as the libido wants to strike out on another path, and for this purpose begins running back along the previous bridges of projection, they will work as the greatest hindrances it is possible to imagine, for they effectively prevent any real detachment from the former object. We then witness the characteristic phenomenon of a person trying to devalue the former object as much as possible in order to detach his libido from it. But as the previous identity is due to the projection of subjective

contents, complete and final detachment can only take place when the imago that mirrored itself in the object is restored, together with its meaning, to the subject. This restoration is achieved through conscious recognition of the projected content, that is, by acknowledging the "symbolic value" of the object.[2]

The concept of projection, however, is a limited one and insufficient to the task of describing our connection to our environment. In searching for a better paradigm Jung rediscovered the Platonic idea of the "Anima Mundi" or "World Soul." Whereas previously Jung had decried the state of entanglement created by our web of projections and participation mystique, now he bemoans the loss of what Gaston Bachelard has called our anthropocosmic ties:

The development of Western philosophy during the last two centuries has succeeded in isolating the mind in its own sphere and in severing it from its primordial oneness with the universe. Man himself has ceased to be the microcosm and eidolon of the cosmos, and his "anima" is no longer the consubstantial scintilla, or spark of the Anima Mundi, the World Soul.[3]

The initial purpose of this essay is not to suggest the preferability of either of these perspectives. One results from a rational empirical approach, while the other belongs to a philosophical tradition considered "speculative" and "mystical" by Western standards. Both, however, agree that a fundamental qualitative change in the relationship of man to his environment has resulted from the development of ego-consciousness. It is the nature of this change, specifically as reflected in humanity's conception of sacred space, which this essay seeks to explore.

When Gilgamesh returns to Uruk and gazes at the magnificent wall which surrounds his city, he momentarily forgets the tragic dimension of his human existence, awed as he is by the suggestion of permanence and majesty latent in mortar and stone.

Humankind has been awed by and expressed its awe in buildings ever since. For those who built them these buildings often provided a vehicle, a conduit, connecting them with the great forces of the Divine. For those of us who study them, these structures and spaces provide a glimpse of humanity's attempt to maintain a relationship that we have lost.

II. Gods in the Landscape

The aborigines of Australia, a nomadic people subsisting on hunting and gathering, have not developed an architecture in the usual sense of this term, for they inhabit no location for very long and their impact on their environment is roughly equivalent to that of other species of similar size and population density. What distinguishes the aborigine is a clearly articulated worldview, centered around a body of stories known collectively as "the dreaming."

> The dreaming is a kind of narrative of things that once happened; a kind of charter of things that still happen; and a kind of logos or principle of order transcending everything significant for aboriginal man.[4]

Connection is made to this transcendental logos through the act of dreaming, suggesting that the Australian aborigine regards the unconscious, as manifested in his dreams, as the source of "ultimate reality."

The stories of the dreaming posit a time of creation when mythic beings emerged from a lifeless and featureless earth. They resembled plants or animals yet behaved like humans. Their activities form the content of this extraordinary body of folklore. When creation time abruptly ended and these strange and marvelous creatures died, they left behind reminders for those to come:

> Each place in which one or another of them had carried out any task or feat, or had acted in some memorable way, is now marked by a natural feature.[5]

The aborigines regard these mythical beings as their ancestors and see their natural surroundings as manifestations of the sacred time of origins,

> so every aboriginal is linked intimately by myth and lineage with everything in his or her environment. Such links dominate every aspect of aboriginal life.[6]

Therefore it is not only through dreams, but also through their relationship with their environment, that aborigines make contact with primordial, generative archetypes. The following quote from C. P. Mountford's *The Dreamtime Book* clearly indicates this relationship:

> There are many tall grotesque human figures painted in the caves of the rugged Kimberley Ranges of north-western Australia. According to tribal beliefs, these paintings are not the work of the aborigines, but of the Wandjina people who lived in that country during the time of creation. Each painting is associated with some particular creature or plant.
>
> At the close of the creation period, each Wandjina painted his own likeness on the wall of a cave, then entered either the rock-face on which he had painted his image, or the water of a nearby spring. At the same time the spirit of the Wandjinas decreed that, with the beginning of every wet season, each painting should be renovated by its associated aborigines. These renovations cause the spirit to impregnate its own special creature or plant, and thus provide an abundance of these foods.[7]

Recalling many analogous rites involving ritual renewal of a god or totem practiced by primitive people worldwide, this example clearly demonstrates the aboriginal's participation in the mythic dimension of his environment. It is especially important to note that these paintings constitute one of the very few modifications of their environment practiced by these nomadic people. Although this activity produces neither physical safety nor shelter, it would be wrong to consider it non-utilitarian, for by it they are assisting in the regeneration of the creative forces inherent in nature.

Ritual renewal is thought by many to be the central meaning behind the neolithic monuments constructed by the Bronze Age inhabitants of the downs of southern England. The calendrical nature of the Stonehenge formation and its significance for the yearly agricultural cycle of death and rebirth are now generally accepted. Vincent Scully has noted that the so-called "Heel Stone" at Stonehenge is "of such a height that its top . . . lies exactly upon the horizon, close to the point where the sun rises on midsummer day. . . ."[8] This does not occur precisely on the solstice, but a few days before and again a few days after. The time between alignments could have marked the beginning and conclusion of an important ritual or festival, as Scully has suggested, celebrating the zenith of nature's productive season. What better way to emphasize the cosmic significance of humanity's activities than to have the sun itself announce the precise limits of ritual time through the medium of architecture?

Stonehenge, however, is not an isolated monument but part of a complex grouping of henges, menhirs, and tumuli. Michael Dames has suggested that the entire sculpted landscape is related to the worship of the Mother Goddess.[9] Thus the barrows, henges, and downs can be seen as representations of the Mother Goddess at various points during her life cycle: child, maiden, lover, pregnant mother, and finally crone. Each year this cycle was celebrated in the appropriate corresponding season. Dames believed that "every enactment of the cycle was definitive and the first. The whole universe was continually being founded in the primordial mythical events which ceaselessly inaugurated existence."[10] Here, as in the rites of the Australian aborigines, the ritual of renewal enacted in relationship to a humanly modified environment involved a return to the events of "the beginning."

Where the people of the downs had to build their own sacred hills and barrows, the ancient Greeks were able to find their gods in the unmodified natural environment. Once thought of as stark, white, abstract forms deliberately set in contrast to nature, the Greek temple—argues Vincent Scully—was very much a part of and a response to, not only the surrounding landscape, but especially the sacred energy residing therein. Scully states that:

> All Greek sacred architecture explores and praises the char-
> acter of a god or group of gods in a specific place. That place is
> itself holy and, before the temple was built upon it, embodied
> the whole of the deity as a recognized natural force.[11]

For the Greeks "the land was not a picture but a true force which physically embodied the powers that ruled the world...."[12]

Scully illustrates his thesis with the siting of Cretan palace architecture, whose early examples are contemporaneous with
the monuments of the English downs. Scully finds in the vast
majority of these palaces a consistent pattern of landscape
elements, including "a gently mounded or conical hill on axis
with the palace to north or south" and a "higher, double-
peaked or cleft mountain some distance beyond the hill but on
the same axis." This double-peaked or notched formation suggests to Scully a pair of horns, a well-known attribute of the
Cretan Mother Goddess. These natural elements are "the basic
architecture of the palace complex. They define its space and
focus it." Together with the manmade elements, these natural
features "create one ritual whole, in which man's part is defined
and directed by the sculptural masses of the land and is subordinate to their rhythms."[13]

Although Scully does not hypothesize any element of renewal
through ritual participation in the environment, he does stress
the importance of the sense of being in contact with and con-
tained in the Goddess herself. For Scully, Cretan architecture

> seems to celebrate the power of the goddess of the earth, of
> whom man, like all other animals, is simply an adjunct, and to
> whose rhythms his whole desire must be to conform.[14]

Another hallowed place which connects landscape to gods
through architecture is India. There "the entire land is . . . a sacred
geometry."[15] Mountain ranges abound in mythic associations,

and just as the Greek gods were said to live on Olympus, so the Hindu gods make their homes in the Himalayas.[16] All the major rivers in India are considered sacred reflections of that most sacred stream, the Ganges, which is said to have once flowed only in heaven before consenting to come to earth.[17] The importance of these rivers is such that "All water used in ritual is symbolically transformed into sacred water by invoking the presence of the Ganghes and other sacred rivers."[18]

Specific places are also considered holy throughout India. These tirthas (sacred fords or crossings) and dhams (divine abodes) are the natural epiphanies of the divine,[19] recalling Eliade's definition of sacred space as the scene of a theophany.

These examples indicate the prevalence of the belief that gods reside in nature and constitute its dynamic principles. Connection with and propitiation of these forces—a vital concern—was accomplished through the practice of ritual in carefully arranged architectural spaces. In India this architectural dimension was of a somewhat different order. Rather than reaching out to include the surrounding landscape in its design, it incorporates manmade reflections of natural forms (whose significances are sacred) in a more self-contained symbolic format.

III. The Delineation of Sacred Space

Calling Indian sacred architecture "self-contained" is not to imply that the site is of little consequence. For instance "the ground on which the temple is to be constructed is carefully selected on the basis of its auspicious situation and seeded for the auspicious sign of germination"—that is, the fertile nature of the location as determined by a rite involving seeding the ground.[21] The temple is self-contained in that, rather than being positioned in relationship to a sacred mountain or landscape, it itself becomes the symbolic expression of a sacred mountain, and "like the mountain, the temple links heaven and earth."[22]

Just as in Greece, Indian temples are built to house the gods. However, here the location does not need to be associated with that god prior to construction, as the consecration invocation implies:

> Let spirits, gods, and demons depart and seek other habita-
> tions. From now on this place belongs to the divinity whose
> temples will be built here.[23]

Indian gods, it seems, are more mobile and less fundamentally attached to specific places than those discussed above. Though the earth still teems with supernatural life, both demonic and divine, these forces are subject to eviction and displacement, provided the proper ritual is followed.

In the design and construction of the temple, "the universe in microcosm is reconstructed."[24] The floor plan is a mandala with the sanctum, the abode of the divine image, at its center. This mandala specifically invokes Purusa, the original person, whose self-sacrifice and dismemberment created the cosmos and gave structure to natural and social reality. Just as Vedic sacrifice is concerned with the reconstruction of Purusa's original whole-ness, so too does a "similar reconstruction of the body-cosmos [occur] . . . in the construction of the Hindu temple."[25] Here we find convincing evidence for Eliade's statement that "construc-tion rituals . . . presuppose the more or less explicit imitation of the cosmogonic act."[26] Once again ritual regeneration of the cosmic forces and return to the "mythical moment of the begin-ning"[27] are evident.

Like the Indian temple, the Temple of Jerusalem constitutes a condensed image of the cosmos. Eliade's description is based upon Flavius Josephus's account:

> . . . the three parts of the sanctuary correspond to the three
> cosmic regions . . . the twelve loaves on the table are the
> twelve months of the year; the candelabrum with seventy
> branches represents the decans. The builders of the Temple
> not only constructed the world, they also constructed cosmic
> time.[28]

This is illustrated by an important feature in the siting of the

Temple of Jerusalem, a feature which recalls the calendrical dimension of Stonehenge:

> . . . it was the first rays of the rising sun upon the morning of the fall equinoctial day, the New Year's day of the solar calendar, shining directly in through the eastern gate of the Temple at Jerusalem, closed tightly all through the year but opened upon just this one day and for this particular occasion, shining in through this eastern gate and down the long axis of the Temple court and building into the debir, the sacred cubicle at the western end of the sanctuary. The temple was so oriented that only upon the two equinoctial days in the year could this phenomenon occur. For a brief moment the rays of the sun penetrated into the innermost recesses of the sanctuary, dark throughout all the remainder of the year, and illumined this with golden radiance, kabod (cf. Isa 60, 1). Then slowly, inch by inch, as the sun rose higher and higher above the Temple, the ray of golden light shortened and receded from the holy place. Soon the sun had risen so high that no more light at all shone into the sacred edifice. Complete darkness has returned, to endure until the next equinoctial New Year's Day, the next opening of the eastern gate.[29]

This occasion carried great significance for the life of the community:

> Originally this day was celebrated as the New Year's Day, the most important festival occasion within the entire year. Upon the proper and punctilious performance of the peculiar and complex ritual by the king himself, the chief religious functionary of the kingdom, or, upon occasion, by his surrogate, the very existence and welfare of the entire nation were thought to depend.[30]

The similarity to Stonehenge is striking, but let us not overlook the differences. Here the relationship to the cosmos is strictly astral, specifically solar; no connection was sought to a chthonic or feminine deity. No terrestrial theophany is expressed.

The forces which animate the cosmos have withdrawn from the immediate environment and have become transcendent, inhabiting only the celestial regions.

This may explain the decisive role of verticality in the sacred architecture of the West. We have already seen how the Indian temple, as sacred mountain, functions as axis mundi, or link between heaven and earth. In Eliade's conception the axis mundi not only ascends to the heavens but also descends to the underworld, connecting all three of the cosmic regions. Somehow this conception lent itself to splitting cosmic energy into its positive and negative poles, with the negative aspect universally relegated to the subterranean region. It was then just a short step to seek to propitiate the celestial realm, while seeking to avoid contact with the infernal realm. That which was in, of, or below the earth became negative and inferior, subject to ritual avoidance, exorcism and, eventually, repression.

Connection to the heavens, however, remained important. Eliade describes in *Shamanism* the widespread cosmology of Siberian Eskimos which conceives of the sky as a tent, held in place like a stake by the Pole Star. This domestic cosmology found expression in

> the microcosm inhabited by mankind. . . . Among the Soyot the pole rises above the top of the yurt and its end is decorated with blue, white, and yellow cloths, representing the colors of the celestial regions. This pole is sacred; it is regarded almost as a god. At its foot stands a small stone altar, on which offerings are placed.[31]

Here the connection is immediate, domestic, and intimate between daily activity and the overarching cosmic principle of order.

We find in ancient Babylonia this idea of an axis mundi embodied in the image of the cosmic mountain or in its manmade substitute, the ziggurat. Siegfried Giedion states that:

> Both ziggurat and pyramid derive their existence from man's
> awakened urge toward the vertical as a symbol of contact with
> the deity, contact with the sky.[32]

Giedion further observes that:

> the organization of the interior space of the temples before
> 3,000 B.C. testified to a desire to attain direct contact with in-
> visible powers with no intermediary aid of anthropomorphic
> deities.[33]

During the elaboration of the ziggurat form, however, "the
devaluation of interior space proceeded step by step, parallel
with the mounting rigidity of the hierarchical social structure."[34]
Although his analysis is based on social considerations, the
transformation in sacred architecture which Giedion detects
tends to confirm the thesis that the displacement of deities to a
heavenly region resulted in a lessening in the experience of
sacred immanence, that is, of the Anima Mundi.

What has been suggested by this analysis of the evolution of
sacred space is a transformation in the experience of divinity, or
cosmic dynamism, from being in and of the world to being
remote from it and how this transformation manifests itself in
architectural form. What remains to be demonstrated is the outcome of this process of transformation in our own times. This
shall be left to the powers of observation of the reader for whom
our modern, secular environment is an everyday experience.
One can still determine vestiges of the architectural expressions
described herein: church steeples still point heavenward,
cathedral doors still open toward the rising sun. One might even
claim that demons still inhabit the earth, waiting to be exorcised
by bulldozer and pile-driver. Humanity's ongoing obsession
with the heavens can be observed in rocket ships and sky-
scrapers, as can the continuing devaluation of the earth in acid
rain and hazardous waste. Could this be an example of what
Jung was referring to when he described "the characteristic
phenomenon of a person trying to devalue the former object as
much as possible in order to detach his libido from it"?

Much of that vitalizing libido seems indeed to have been detached, for the fundamental fact of our modern relationship to our environment remains that we are, in the words of Enkidu:

> left alone, unable to understand
> In a world where nothing lives anymore
> As you thought it did.
> Nothing like yourself, everything like dead
> Clay. . . . [35]

IV. Postscript and Prescriptions

Let us look again at Jung's statement on projection quoted in the preface. Preeminently in the worldview of the Australian aborigine do we find an example of what Jung calls a "compulsive, i.e. 'magical' or 'mystical'" system of projections which binds a person to his environment. The most basic value in aboriginal society is conservative: to imitate and perpetuate the eternal conditions of the dreamtime. No change in behavior can be sanctioned, for this would imply a departure from the original and authentic archetypal patterns. By modern standards this is compulsive indeed. Yet this example is only one of many illustrating what Eliade considers to be a fundamental "primitive" ontological conception:

> an object or an act becomes real only insofar as it imitates or repeats an archetype. Thus, reality is acquired solely through repetition or participation; everything which lacks an exemplary model is "meaningless", i.e., it lacks reality. [36]

Thus the ritual interaction of humankind with the environment, or with the archetypes perceived or projected therein, serves to preserve the sense of meaning required for social and psychic cohesion. In *The Sacred and the Profane* Eliade tells the story of an Australian group whose most sacred object was a tall pole which represented the tribe's connection to the ancestors and the forces of nature. The pole went everywhere with this nomadic group, constituting the literal as well as the metaphoric focal point and unifying symbol of social and psychic order. When the pole became broken by some unspecified accident, the aborigines wandered about aimlessly. Then one by one they lay down on the ground to wait for the death they felt sure would result from this catastrophic event. No life, at least no truly vital and meaningful life, was conceivable to these people without their connection to archetypal reality.

Within the parameters of such a compulsive and undifferentiated connection to the environment, any possibility for the expansion of consciousness is limited. Thus is the withdrawal of projections generally considered to be a prerequisite for psychic growth. The individual in the process of change is challenged to find his own internal relationship to the projected content.

The conflict this challenge engenders, as in the crisis of adolescence, often requires a devaluation of the outer 'object' in an attempt to loosen the bonds of projection. The mother, for instance, can no longer remain the all-nurturing source of comfort and sustenance, for she now stands in the path of the child's need to become a self-reliant adult. Therefore her archetypal complexion changes for the youth: either she is now devalued from her previous archetypal glorification, or else the negative mother archetype is constellated and a heroic battle to slay the dragon ensues. In both cases the archetypal backdrop constitutes the critical ingredient in the quality of the relationship. "Projection," or the contamination of 'objective' reality with subjective contents, remains constant. Even the resolution of the adolescent crisis by no means need imply an end to projection. Most people simply find other vehicles to carry the archetypal functions of mother and father, whether in job, church, alma mater, or philosophical system.

According to Jung release from this state of entanglement

> can only take place when the imago that mirrored itself in the object is restored, together with its meaning, to the subject. This restoration is achieved through conscious recognition of the projected content, that is, by acknowledging the "symbolic value" of the object.[37]

Jung's conclusion here implies that when projection is recognized one does not discard the object as being of no further use. Rather its value has been paradoxically enhanced by its recognition as a symbol, the carrier of psychic meaning. This, for Jung, is no longer projection but an important and conscious use of externals to reflect internal truths.

It remains to be demonstrated how this process can be effected without shattering the symbolic vehicle, like the aborigine's sacred pole, and thereby severing the all-important relationship to the source of meaning. Perhaps this concern is irrelevant, for, as Hayden Carruth has noted, we live in a "world from which first the spirit, then history, and finally nature have fled."[38] The problem, then, is to reestablish communication with these essential forces. Where can we now turn for what has been aptly described as "a poetic vision of the cosmos which fulfills the soul's need for placing itself in the vast scheme of things"?[39]

The importance placed by a variety of cultures on the theme of regeneration and return to the original time of creation has been demonstrated. What this ritualistic emphasis suggests is that humanity has a vital role to play in the perpetuation and recreation of the primordial life-giving principles, the archetypes. Without human participation in this regenerative process, the archetypal forces "indwelling in the world" will cease bestowing meaning on our relationship to the world. The world will, in effect, die by virtue of our failure to recognize our participation in and identity with the stream of life that runs through all creation. This is, in fact, a very accurate characterization of our current environmental predicament.

In this regard Jung has stated that

> ... it is the function of consciousness not only to recognize and assimilate the external world through the gateway of the senses, but to translate into visible reality the world within us.[40]

This internal world is composed of the eternal archetypes, whose periodic constellations and regenerations form the meaningful basis of all psychic life. Withdrawing projections is only part of the problem of individuation. In addition, humankind needs a creative interaction with the natural and manmade environments which allows symbolic meaning to be carried by physical objects, by buildings, and by the space they inhabit. This is not an interaction alien to the natural functioning of the human psyche, as our examples have shown.

The "primitive" believes that his life has meaning, and his community and world have life, only insofar as they relate to the archetypal paradigms which exist in eternity. Perhaps this relationship constitutes the eternal life sought by Gilgamesh and for which we must continue to seek in our efforts to renew a meaningful rapport with "the divine life indwelling in the world."

1. *Gilgamesh: A Verse Narrative*, rendered by Herbert Mason (New York: New American Library, 1972), 92.

2. C. G. Jung, *CW* 8, § 507.

3. C. G. Jung, *CW* 11, § 759.

4. W. E. H. Stanner, "The Dreaming: An Australian World View," in *Cultural and Social Anthropology: Selected Readings*, ed. Peter Hammond (New York: MacMillan Co., 1964), 289.

5. Charles P. Mountford, *The Dreamtime Book: Australian Aboriginal Myths* (Adelaide: Rigby Ltd., 1973), 3.

6. Ibid.

7. Ibid., 30.

8. Vincent Scully, *The Earth, the Temple, and the Gods: Greek Sacred Architecture* (New Haven: Yale University Press, 1962), 24.

9. Michael Dames, *The Avebury Cycle* (London: Thames and Hudson, 1977), 9.

10. Ibid., 15. Quoted from F. DeGraeve, *The New Catholic Encyclopedia*, vol. 10, 1968, 183.

11. Scully, *The Earth, the Temple*, 1.

12. Ibid., 3.

13. Ibid., 11.

14. Ibid., 18.

15. Diana L. Eck, *Darsan: Seeking the Divine Image in India* (Chambersburg, Pa.: Anima Publications, 1981), 48.

16. Ibid.

17. Ibid., 49.

18. Ibid.

19. Ibid., 3.

20. Mircea Eliade, *The Myth of the Eternal Return or, Cosmos and History* (Princeton: Princeton University Press, 1954), 4.

21. Eck, *Darsan*, 44.

22. Ibid., 46.

23. Ibid., 44. Quoted from Stella Kramrisch, *The Hindu Temple*, 2 vols. (1946; reprint, Delhi: Motilal Banarsidass, 1976), 13.

24. Ibid.

25. Ibid., 45.

26. Eliade, *Myth of Eternal Return*, 76.

27. Ibid., 77.

28. Ibid., 77-78.

29. Julian Morgenstern, *The Fire upon the Altar* (Chicago: Quadrangle Book, 1963), 70.

30. Ibid.

31. Mircea Eliade, *Shamanism: Archaic Techniques of Ecstasy* (Princeton: Princeton University Press, 1964), 261.

32. Siegfried Giedion, *The Beginnings of Architecture* (Princeton: Princeton University Press, 1964), 219.

33. Ibid., 214.

34. Ibid., 191.

35. Mason, *Gilgamesh*, 49.

36. Eliade, *Myth of Eternal Return*, 34.

37. See note 2.

38. Hayden Carruth, *Working Papers: Selected Essays and Reviews* (Athens: University of Georgia Press, 1982), 93.

39. James Hillman, "*Anima Mundi*: The Return of the Soul to the World," *Spring 1982*: 82.

40. C. G. Jung, *CW* 8, §342.

CONSTRUCTION (de)CONSTRUCTION (re)CONSTRUCTION
Failed Attempts at Healing an Irreparable World

STANLEY TIGERMAN

The (pre)Text of American (forget)Fulness

The Amnesiac (pre)*Text* for an American Absence—or exile —(under)*writes*—or (under)*rights*—tries to heal the wounds of nostalgia, exile, and death. Failed attempts come from an (in)*ability* to cleanse the contamination seeded at the garden of Eden. Humankind's determination to heal the (un)*healable*—to bear the (un)*bearable*—is the result of a desire to (re)*store* innocence. This insistence leads to attempts to deflect life's trajectory away from its inevitable, (ir)*reducible* end. Nostalgia about intersecting with divinity grounds a *construction* of mimesis. Frustration with humankind's (in)*ability* to overcome exile leads to the apocalyptic (de)*construction* of an (un)*equal* relationship. Failed attempts to (dis)*place* death are the constituency of (re)*construction*.

Member* 1	(dis)Member** 2	(re)Member
Construction	(de)Construction	(re)Construction
Zimzum	Shevirath	Tikkun
	Hakelim	

*If the six-pointed star is an ancient symbol for healing, why does "time heal all wounds"?

**Members* of the (in)*human* race are (dis)*member*ed through their participation in, observation—or acknowledgment of—a holocaust, which they all (sub)/(un)*consciously* (re)*member*. At Masada, in memory of its fall, initiated *member*s of the Israeli army (re)*member* (dis)*member*ment by swearing the oath "Never again."

The (sub)Text of Kabbalistic Interpretation[1]

Zimzum *   *Shevirath*   *Tikkun* * * *
                 Hakelim * *

*Zimzum is the Creator's withdrawal or contraction to make possible a creation (*member*) that is not (him)*self*. * *Shevirath Hakelim is the breaking-apart-of-the-vessels ([dis]*member*), a vision of creation-as-catastrophe. * * *Tikkun is restitution or restoration ([re]*member*)—man's contribution to God's work.

1. Member—n. 1. A person belonging to an incorporated or organized body, society, etc.: a member of Congress, a member of a club. 2. A limb or other functional organ of an animal body. 3. A part or element of a structural or composite whole, distinguishable from other parts or elements, as a part of a sentence, syllogism, period, or discourse, or any necessary part of a structural framework, as a tie rod, post, or strut in the truss of a bridge. 4. A subordinate classificatory part: A species is a member of a genus. 5. Bot. A part of a plant considered with reference to position and structure, but regardless of function. 6. Math. a. Either side of an equation. b. A set of figures or symbols forming part of a formula or number. c. Any one of the items forming a series.

2. Dis-member—v. 1. To cut or pull limb from limb or part from part. 2. To divide; separate into parts and distribute, as an empire.

3. Re-member—v. 1. To bring back or present again to the mind or memory; recall; recollect. 2. To keep in mind carefully, as for a purpose. 3. To bear in mind with affection, respect, awe,

etc. 4. To bear in mind as worthy of a reward, gift, etc.: She remembered me in her will. 5. To reward; tip: Remember the steward. 6. Obs. To remind. 7. To have or use one's memory.

Modernism	(post)*Modernism*	(re)Post- *modernism* (Riposte)
Construction	(de)*Construction*	(re)*Construction*
Production 1	Destruction	(re)*Production* 2
Present 3	Absent	(re)*Present* 4

1. Production—n. 1. The act or process of producing. 2. In political economy, a producing for use, involving the creating or increasing of economic wealth: in contradistinction to consumption (by use). 3. That which is produced or made; any tangible result of industrial, artistic, or literary labor.

2. Re-production—n. 1. The act or power of reproducing. 2. Biol. The process by which an animal or plant gives rise to another of its kind; generation. 3. Psychol. *The process of the memory by which objects that have previously been known are brought back into consciousness* (emphasis is mine). 4. That which is reproduced, as a revival in drama or a copy in art.

3. Present—adj. 1. Being in a place or company referred to or contemplated; being at hand; opposed to absent. 2. Now going on; current; not past or future. 3. Actually in mind. 4. Immediately impending or actually going on; not delayed; instant. 5. Relating to or signifying what is going on at the time being; the present tense, present participle. 6. Ready at hand; prompt in emergency; a present wit, a present aid. n. 1. Present time; now; the time being. 2. Gram. The present tense; also, a verbal form denoting it. 3. A present matter or affair; a question under consideration. 4. Pl. law. Present writings: term for the document in which the word occurs: Know all men by these presents.

4. Re-present—v.t. 1. To serve as the symbol, expression or designation of; symbolize: The letters of the alphabet represent

the sounds of speech. 2. To express or symbolize in this manner: to represent royal power with a scepter. 3. To set forth a likeness or image of; depict; portray, as in painting or sculpture. 4. a. To produce on the stage, as an opera. b. To act the part of; impersonate, as a character in a play. 5. To serve as or be the delegate, agent, etc., of: He represents the State of Maine. 6. To describe as being of a specified character or condition: They represented him as a genius. 7. To set forth in words; state; explain: He represented the circumstances of his case. 8. To bring before the mind; present clearly. 9. To serve as an example, specimen, type, etc., of; typify: His use of words represents an outmoded school of writing.

Structuralism	(post)_Structuralism_	(re)_Poststructuralism_
		Riposte _Structuralism_
		(re)_Claim_*
		(re)_Cover_*
		(re)_New_*
		(re)_Store_*

The (con)Text of the Initial Wound (Original Sin)

*Acknowledging the presence of a wound (and expressing that admission by [re]_presenting_ that lesion [cut, coup] by the scar that signifies it) does not relieve one from the responsibility that accompanies and defines human behavior. It is natural to expect attempts to heal the wound. Even so, it is impossible to overcome the knowledge that the wound can never be cured without plastic surgery, which means the suppression of the memory of the first wound that defines all following wounds (self-inflicted amnesia)—i.e., faith—assuring its (dis)_appearance_. The original wound is of three stages: (1) the fall from a state of grace in paradise, (2) exile from that divine garden, and (3) death. These require recognition; they demand attention —not suppression.

Recognition of the first stage results in a nostalgic attitude so as to retrieve an (ir)*retrievable* innocence. Recognition of the second stage results in resistance to the agony of exile, shown by a determination to search for the lost home. Recognition of the third stage results in a rejection of death. The commonality of response to each stage is driven by making the opposite equal to each original position.

Faith renders any interpretation of the original wound (un)*necessary*, thereby muting memory. Finally, the same faith nullifies any responsibility to (re)*write*—indeed to (re)*right* —that original failure without (re)*moving* it from memory. Rather than acting out mimetic iterations through repetition, Americans try to (re)*produce* originary evidence, so as to "get it right" the next time; even though they know (sub)*consciously* that "it" can neither be "righted," nor can one ever "get it right." Americans try (even though they fail) to (re)*gain* lost time (never thinking they may be out of time), by yearning for an intersection with lost origins, for an absent beginning.

(re)*Presentation* infers a better time, as belief in a present tempered by a future can be seen as an opportunity to make things better (i.e., to gain lost time). (re)*Presentation* is rationalized by superimposing the concept of time on the present. While it is within the definitive ethics of architecture to try to do this, the knowledge that failure is always imminent has only marginal acceptance within architectural traditions. These are the same traditions that mute the memory of original sin. After all, architecture has long served systems that validate the (dis)*appearance* of the problem (i.e., perpetual value systems). Otherwise, Plato could never have accused it (art) of being in the shadow of truth.

(re)*Production* verifies belief in the original product. (re)*Production* is an admission that the product has value by trying to make it better by repeatedly (re)*making* it (the purpose of cross-fertilization). Indeed, the purpose underlying the conceiving of a child implies that the next generation will be better than the one before. (re)*Production* uses the passage of time to heal the wound of the entrance into the world of a (re)*produced* product. And the idea of attempting to improve a situation contradicts the cynical view that (no)*thing* ever gets better—it is only different. This is where cross-fertilization intersects with architecture. Each is seminally informed by the optimism in both: I take this optimism to signify attempts at healing.

"While Hegel maintains that when love is truly conceived, 'the wounds of spirit heal and leave no scars,' Heidegger insists that the rending of difference can never be totally healed."

    *Belief**   (dis)*Belief***   (re)*lief****

                                                       (Re)*new*ed Belief

*With Hegel, a long onto-theological tradition comes to an end, through "synthesis" (or is it [sin]*Thesis?*)—a mechanism that suborns "thesis" and suppresses "(anti)*thesis*," in favor of (re)*solving* and presumably amalgamating both. The "scab" of antithesis is allowed to heal (the scar of synthesis reluctantly retains the palimpsest of the scab of antithesis). Plastic surgery (in the guise of faith made manifest in synthesis) removes the trace of the wound of (anti)*thesis*, whose presence would otherwise be (un)*bearable* in its (un)*resolved* perpetuation, indeed in its insistent (re)*interpretation*. For Hegel, no further interpretation of the sacred text is required; faith—or belief—first (dis)*places*, then (re)*places* exegesis, since the contravention of (anti)*thesis* is removed. Textuality ceases to be an irritation—(anti)*thesis*, and with it interpretation, is (dis)*placed* into a hiatic state of limbo, awaiting (re)*activation*.

**Americans inherit a post-Nietzschean world where first the sacred other—God—then the sacred self—man—is murdered. Belief in a divine being and in any being is (dis)*placed* by (dis)*belief*. Self is (re)*placed* by an equal "otherness" in an (un)*solvable* equation (un)*burdened* by ethical considerations. Originally, the sacred other and the sacred self were on opposite sides of the equation, where, by each needing the other, a false state of parity was induced. The introduction of (dis)*belief* (dis)*locates* the original equation and, with that (dis)*locative* introduction, (dis)*places* parity, just as it (dis)*places* first God and then man in a place that is (no)*place*.

***Born of other strains, the attempt to produce one better than the original through cross-fertilization is called "hybrid" or "child."

Belief	(dis)*Belief*	(re)*lief*
		(re)*New*ed
Vest	(di)Vest	(re)Vest
Tract	(dis)Tract	(re)Tract
Tort	(dis)Tort	(re)Tort
Solve	(de)Solve	(re)Solve
Sign	(de)Sign	(re)Sign
Assemble	(dis)Semble	(re)Semble
Prove	(dis)Prove	(re)Prove
Plenish	(de)Plenish	(re)Plenish
Orient	(dis)Orient	(re)Orient
Generate	(de)Generate	(re)Generate
Inform	(de)Form	(re)Form
Fit	(mis)Fit	(re)Fit
Direct	(mis)Direct	(re)Direct
Claim	(dis)Claim	(re)Claim
Compose	(de)Compose	(re)Compose
Cast	(mis)Cast	(re)Cast
Reading	(mis)Reading	(re)Reading
Appropriate	(mis)Appropriate	(re)Appropriate
Count	(dis)Count	(re)Count
Course	(dis)Course	(re)Course
Centering	(de)Centering	(re)Centering
Nomination	(de)Nomination	(re)Nomination
Location	(dis)Location	(re)Location
Placement	(dis)Placement	(re)Placement
Construction	(de)*Construction*	(re)*Construction*

Cover	(dis)Cover	(re)Cover
Evaluation	(de)Valuation	(re)Valuation
Activate	(de)Activate	(re)Activate
Formation	(de)Formation	(re)Formation
Home²	*Exile³*	*Home Away From Home⁴*

The (re)Pressed Text of American Architecture

As the twentieth century nears its end, it is becoming clear that the (im)*possible* search for an American architecture has been (dis)*located* in a time marked by time (marking time) and at a place signifying (no)*place* of (im)*probable* closure. This reveals a (dis)*junction* symbolic of the site of an American absence (re)*presenting* an empty inheritance originally learned just outside Eden's east gate. The first element that expresses the features of any epoch—language—is currently (de)*limited* in despair by utterances (dis)*located* from both theocentric and anthropocentric values.

Linguistic codes exert power through expression and suppression. They influence (im)*measurably* the elements that they define. (de)*Coded*, like Samson bald, they appear to state facts even as they reveal the magic of the moment.

In America, a land made up of exiles, the desire to return to an original state of innocence (as a [re]*placement* for the failure to live in an alien land which resists "rooting") now has a corresponding set of linguistic codes that are used to express our time's (dis)*junctive* nature. Denials (dis)*place* originary definitions that rooted mankind to being and existence through dwelling in a home always at home. The cynicism of sophistication (age) has (re)*placed* the spontaneity of innocence (youth). In a new, child-like America, before its fall from grace, it was not always that way. The (co)*incidence* between the optimism of a young nation and a discipline such as architecture, whose traditions ring with optimism, is understood. This (co)*incidence* is powered by the courage to accept a belief system (re)*activated* by "newness."

Modernism may have begun in the Renaissance as an appropriation, but it was never enjoyed (nor exploited) more than by a nation of self-consciously innocent exiles who, if they were to be true to their optimism, had to (re)*direct* their condition constructively in "modern ways." The very word—*Modernism*—implies a state of amnesia about the past, a determined attachment to the present, while tilting slightly to the future. Dialectically, however, Modernism is also a challenge to a (pre)*Modern* state which inadvertently clarifies modernism while appearing to stand over and against it. Modernism found a home in a childlike, youthful America free from cunning, (un)*informed* by deceit, (un)*tainted* by sophistication. It dwelt in an America for whom the present meant everything and where (forget)*fulness* about history seemed essential to young Americans schizophrenically revealed in their (pre)*mimetic* innocence, even as they wanted parity with others who, they hoped, saw them as the newest sophisticates.

The (text)Ure of Antinomy

A synthesis ([sin]*Thesis*) of (un)*resolved* (op)*positions* based on the (ir)*reconcilability* of necessary inferences or conclusions (antinomy) seems (un)*likely* in an age devoted either to self-verification through the uses of the past or to an (un)*conditional* indulgence in the future's (un)*predictability*. Both strategies (dis)*locate* a belief in the power of the present. The resulting ambivalence elevates (dis)*junction* to a position of domination. It suggests that the quality of presence has an (un)*resolvably* slippery Janus face that looks backward and forward, but is so waferlike it cannot speak of its own time. The sound from the masked face of the present is either Babel-like or mute, giving way alternatively to the past's cacophony and/or to the future's vast silences. Simultaneously, by speaking (dis)*cordantly* of other times and other places, the voice of the contemporary is strangled. We seem (un)*able* to articulate a present paradoxically (de)*void* of the inspiration to "blow its own horn."

We should know that looking backward for verification results in the frustration of an exile yearning for an (ir)*re-trievable* innocence, attainable only in memory and (un)*fulfilled* desire.[5] (Op)*positionally,* we should understand that, by "throwing the baby out with the bathwater,"[6] a future without its past is only fictively compelling (and even that is temporary). We are also (re)*minded* that "we (can)*not* not know history."[7] Both polar positions are (un)*promising* since neither is possible (with)*out* knowledge of the other. Each is contaminated by its (op)*posite*; thus neither is innocent. Bookended by positions which describe a condition of antinomy, the present is drained of itself, shifting its weight slightly so that it lies always just out of reach. "Movement" or "mobility" (the oscillation between [op]*positions*) becomes the currency of the contemporary's otherwise vacuous state.

Perhaps today's America is not a generative source of architecture. An absent American architecture may be due to the fact that this country is neither old enough to legitimate, nor young enough to retrieve, visions located elsewhere. On the one hand, America's absence may be tied to the power of its pluralistic precedents which are rooted to a place that is multitudinously "other" than any single one that could be called "home." The power of originary evidence to which many Americans yearn (and with it the [re]*iterative* power of mimesis) overwhelms senses tied to an (other)*wise* (dis)*illusioning* present. On the other hand, by thrusting one's self into the (un)-*known* without the (re)*assurance* of precedent (to say nothing of convention's comfort), the (dis)*junctiveness* of that time's thinness is (re)*enforced* and continues an *absent present.*

The search for a point of origination in order to project form metaphorized by the Edenic tree of life is, in America, a "Faery Land"[8] without roots. It is perhaps even without a native soil which would nourish thoughts of "home," "dwelling," or "being." It is in response to being an American in an age when abundance is characterized by removal from "playing the game" that causes one's gaze to stray to places and pleasures behind, or in front of, one's position in time and place. The suspension of belief in an American presence dislocates value as well as illusion in the power, indeed the existence, of a perpetual American dream. That particular (dis)*junction* (re)*locates* the power of the performer of presence to the selections of the spectator of absence, which results in the domination of the voyeur over the player.

Thus the energy (or is it enervation?) of contemporary (dis)*location* is bracketed by a never-to-be-retrieved past and a never-to-be-fulfilled future. The inference that a (dis)*junctive* present is inevitable is seeded by the (im)*possibility* of fulfillment by moving either forward or backward. It also (re)*enforces* a pause marked by (de)*constructive* marginalia. The death of God combines with the death of man (fore)*closing* whatever optimism might be intrinsic to a *present* that has *presence*. The absence of either "ethical norms or moral forms"[9] conveys a chimeric freedom that exploits the loss of the power of presence. Instead, this imaginary (dis)*closure* presents a contaminated closure signifying the illusion that (im)*perfection* is its own reward—the paradox of the absent present: (de)*construction*.

By elevating interpretation to an (un)*precedented* level of (dis)*belief* (or freedom), not only is faith exacerbated, but ethics are excised in a country needing values in order to mark its maturity. The absence of ethical values (super)*imposed* on a state of incessant interpretation projects a false sense of (in)*dependence* (in)*consistent* with the development of an individual or collective self.

If Hegel's (pro)*position* of the trinity (first Greek, [dis]*placed* by Jew, and [re]*placed* by Christian) is modified ... so that the original, (un)*tampered* belief in *god*(s) is (dis)*placed* by (in) *humanity's* challenge to God through the elevation of the self in order to talk with God (the wound of continuous interpretation), and when that fails and (in)*humanity* is expelled from paradise, then a (pro)*position* (re)*placing* "faith" (plastic surgery) occurs. "There is a theological point of view which says that Western consciousness after the coming of Christ will not again be in immediate contact with the sources of mythical being.''[10] By dislocating Hegel's tripartite (pro)*position* from convention, the potential for contemporary myth-making is revealed. "Christianity in its aspiration to the truth, rather than in myth or tale, has cut us off from the power to create new myth or symbolic constellations adequate to our condition which would be as expressive as those we have inherited from the classical past.''[11] In order to understand the contemporary as a mythological and symbolic source, it is necessary to reopen the original wound.

The palimpsest of the original wound is revealed—an erasure's trace—made by the presence of a scar which (re)*presents* the signature, or name, by which the *attempt* at healing becomes evident. Time is crucial to the understanding of healing, for without the passing of time, humankind's (in)*ability* to sustain pain would not exist, resulting in an (un)*endurable*, continuous pain. The passage of time (combined with [in]*humanity's* amnesia about it) allows for a scab to metamorphose into a scar. Since the mind cannot sustain pain, a scar is a mark that can be interpreted as signifying original pain, while at the same time the scar (re)*presents* the erasure of that pain.

The original wound can never be healed by removal, but an attempt at (re)*conciliation* is necessary to (re)*present* faith in being, existing, dwelling. The scar remains so that one may never forget that there was a wound. A scar bears the trace of a scab troubled by time. A scab (re)*presents* the initial sign of the process of healing or closure as it is engaged by time. When a scab is ripped off, the wound that it marked is (re)*opened*, new blood is shed, and the original pain is (re)*membered*. A scar cannot be (re)*opened* without the creation of a new wound (super)*imposed* by new pain, but its presence (re)*members* the member that was originally ruptured in (dis)*memberment*. Time is crucial to a healing that begins by rupturing a (pre)*existing* condition and ends with the memory of the enactment of a failed attempt to (re)*enliven* that lost, originary pain.

The (sub)Text (super)Imposed on the (con)Text

The correlation between the Lurianically interpreted Kabbalis-tical triptych (*Zimzum, Shevirath Hakelim, Tikkun*) and their architectural counterparts (*construction*, [de]*construction*, [re]-*construction*) cannot be ignored. "The closest aesthetic equiv-alent to Lurianic Contraction is 'limitation,' in the sense that certain images limit meaning more than they restore or repre-sent meaning. Breaking-apart-of-the-vessels is like the aesthetic breaking-apart and replacing of one form by another, which im-agistically is a process of substitution. 'Tikkun,' the Lurianic restitution, is already almost a synonym for 'representation' itself."[12]

The history of Western architecture is stained by an optimism traced by constructive attitudes signified by construction. (in)-*Formed* by anthropocentrism, architects have obligated them-selves mimetically to repeat the paradisaic (un)*equal* hierarch-ical relationship. They subordinate self to that first perfect architect—God—by whose hand man's initial, and only ideal, home —the garden of Eden—was conceived. Traditionally, the desire to "get it right" has been (re)*presented* by buildings sup-pressing any trace of a "wound" or (re)*pressing* the passage of time and—with it—suppressing the only hope of healing that wound. The sign of intrinsic optimism was manifest in construc-tion (i.e., the belief in existence that the Bible, later [re]*written* by Heidegger, addresses).

Whatever the nature of construction—its style, its context, its bias—the optimism of the human spirit innocently, if (in)*ad-vertently*, suppressed "mistakes," so as to mimetically express mankind's (un)*equal* and (im)*perfect* relationship to a divine being. Equal to Lurian's Kabbalistical interpretation of "Zim-zum" (God's withdrawal, making way for mankind), anthro-pocentrism was effected (i.e., the inference of mankind's assum-ing "center stage" to better act out this primary [in]*equality*). Zimzum can be interpreted as God's establishment of authority in Eden through the divine denial "do not eat of the tree in the center of the garden," which by God's withdrawal left "center stage" to Adam and Eve where they could (dis)*obey*. Either way, Adam and Eve are presented a message by God (un)*alterably* demanding a response. God's withdrawal makes Adam's and Eve's presence possible. By responding Adam and Eve establish their own presence—or parity with the divine being—which signifies God's absence—or His withdrawal.

Similarly, the establishing of a corresponding architecture —one that responds mimetically to Eden—not only commits architecture to an (im)*perfect* condition, but ironically (re)*moves* the trace of that (im)*perfection* as it suppresses any possibility of erring in favor of "getting it right." The nature of architecture since that time is couched in the (pre)*tension* of the architect trying to get it right by reducing the passage of time to a condition of absence—conscious removal.

As an architectural analogue to "Zimzum," and as an epilogue to the passion play of Christianity, the architect takes a position of presence—a kind of divine (re)*placement*—so as to "create" mimetically derived iterations of an imagined innocent state equated with perfection. For almost two thousand years, architects have denied the "trace" of that wound which nostalgically draws (in)*humanity* back to an originally innocent state (im)*possible* to attain, (il)*logical* to conceive. Architects strive to reduce the distance between the problems of mimesis as they try to concretize divine ideals into a never to be achieved innocence.

God's withdrawal allows (in)*humanity* to (dis)*place* Him and by (re)*placement* attempt to accomplish similar goals. With the coming of Christianity, faith or belief in an ideal (re)*enforces* architects' resolve as they try to (re)*place* a heavenly garden inhabited by "named"—or known—creatures with a mimetically conceived divine city resurrecting (in)*humanity* from the fall.

Anthropocentric (re)*placement* of a divine being puts (dis)-*place*ment into place. Architecturally, that (dis)*place*ment has a correlation associated with (de)*construction*. Fascinated by strategies embedded in (dis)*junction*, architects adopt devices such as "rupture," "shear," and (un)*resolved* "layering" in order to make architectural correspondence with linguistic (dis)*locations* express today's violence. Therefore, contemporary architectural (dis)*locative* strategies relate to the second stage of Lurianically interpreted Kabbalah—Shevirath Hakelim.

The "breaking-of-the-vessels," an apocalyptic version of creation, explodes the anthropocentric (re)*placement* that occurred as an appropriation conditioned by divine withdrawal. While apocalyptic architecture may seem appropriate to an age marked by (dis)*location* as a sign of violence, the absence of ethics in a discipline otherwise signified by optimism trivializes (in)*humanity's* constructive search for meaning. Not to try to "put Humpty-Dumpty back together again" (no matter how [im] *possible* the task) is to deny being. And that is why Tikkun (i.e., the [in]*escapable* destination of tripartite Lurianic Kabbalah) is so crucial to understand.

To try "restitution" through restorative attempts at "healing" is not only crucial architecturally, it is inevitable from an (in)*human* point of view. Nonetheless, (dis)*locationality* must be recognized as well. The resulting paradox can be seen as a mechanism in order to correlate the (un)*resolvability* of our cultural state with an architecture expressive of that condition.

While Christian faith is the synthesizing element in Hegel's tripartite philosophical project (first Greek, then Jew, and finally Christian), it can be perceived as the first in a new tripartite series (Zimzum), followed by the apocalyptic view of the world metamorphosed by the "breaking-of-the-vessels" (Shevirath Hakelim), and concluded by failed attempts to heal an irreparable wound (Tikkun).

1.   From Harold Bloom's interpretation of Lurianic Kabbalistic typology: *A Map of Misreading* (New York and Cambridge: Oxford University Press, 1975), 5 (parentheses are my own).

2.   Heideggerian version of "Bauen," "Bilded," "Bilden."

3.   See *The Architecture of Exile* by Stanley Tigerman (New York: Rizzoli, 1988).

4.   Replacement of a displaced place.

5.   See my comments on the subject of exile in *The Architecture of Exile*.

6.   A comment normally attributed to Robert A.M. Stern, by way of his justifying Post-Modernist attempts at retrieving the "lost language" (classicism) of architecture.

7.   A comment made by Philip Johnson at a lecture at the Yale School of Architecture in the 1950s.

8. A metaphor employed by A. Bartlett Giametti in his book *Exile and Change in Renaissance Literature* (New Haven: Yale University Press, 1984), relating the condition of foundlings, or orphans, in America to Spenser's *The Faery Queen*.

9. See Giametti's *Exile and Change*.

10. From *The Ecology of Consciousness*, "What Thou Lovest Well Remains," by George Steiner, in *Insight*, July/August 1983.

11. Ibid.

12. Harold Bloom, *A Map of Misreading*, 5, 6.

WORTHWHILE

Jung, C. G. *Nietzsche's Zarathustra*. Ed. James L. Jarrett. Princeton: Princeton University Press, 1988. Two volumes, pp. 1574. $99.50, cloth.

If Freud was Jung's starting point into the depths of the psyche, Nietzsche was his polestar (perhaps even as a student at the University of Basel), beyond (or at) which point lay personal madness, unscientific thinking, wretched excess, and everything else in life and imagination that an explorer of soul who wanted to stay "professional" had to be wary of. The Nietzsche Seminars (1934–1939) are therefore a treasure, certainly for what Jung has to say about Nietzsche, even for what Nietzsche's works say about Jung, but especially for what the reader can glimpse of the constraints imposed on the interplay between such a Master (Nietzsche) and such an inspired reader (Jung). (Freud told an astonished Jung that he had never read Nietzsche. The field, entirely, was Jung's.)

There are the inevitable cautions to the spirit here (these are, after all, the 1930s), and there is the ubiquitous modernist sense of before (our enlightened psychological present) and after, and Jung insists almost ponderously on a vigilant alertness throughout—but there is also that remarkable gift he had for making his reading so compelling to others. Indeed, these volumes are a gold mine for the contemporary interest in the psychology of reading. It will be a rare day when anything so extensive as this act of reading turns up again. For this is neither literary criticism nor philosophy, and least of all a psychoanalytical reading of Nietzsche. It is an amazing document in the history of reading itself.

"But he was a child of his time; he did not know psychology. If he had known what we know nowadays probably his case would have been better, I don't know. We always must recognize, however, that we would not know what we know today if Nietzsche had not lived. Nietzsche has taught us a lot. When I read *Zarathustra* for the first time as a student of twenty-three, of course I did not understand it all, but I got a tremendous impression. I could not say it was this or that, though the poetical beauty of some of the chapters impressed me, but particularly the strange *thought* got hold of me. He helped me in many respects, as many other people have been helped by him. Therefore, we cannot say he should have done differently; we only must remember, if we take it to ourselves, that in reading *Zarathustra*, we must apply certain criticism, for it is very clear where Nietzsche went the wrong way. Otherwise one is simply affected by that identification, because we all suffer from the prejudice of the spirit; of course, it is wonderful to identify with that thing which becomes spiritual, but when we study Nietzsche critically, we see the dangers" (vol. 1, 544).

The words apply to any great writer, of course—indeed, to any great reading. Inspired readers of Jung himself, take note. (CB)

Van Meurs, Jos, with John Kidd. *Jungian Literary Criticism 1920–1980: An Annotated, Critical Bibliography of Works in English*. Metuchen, New Jersey: The Scarecrow Press, 1988. Pp. 288. $32.50, cloth.

This is a useful compendium consisting of 902 alphabetized entries, from Karl Abenheimer's 1945 essay in a British medical journal on King Lear's narcissism ("a convincing psychological perspective of important aspects of Lear") to Carolyn Zonailo's 1980 piece in *Dragonflies* on "The Beast in the Jungle" ("a most perceptive analysis that brings out the subtle shades of moral ambiguity and psychological finesse in one of James' finest stories"). Van Meurs can be critical: "How much more subtle is Shakespeare's psychology than Kirsch's Jungian version of it" (James Kirsch, *Shakespeare's Royal Self*). But often he is not critical enough: "Yet this Jungian reading [June K. Singer, *The Unholy Bible: A Psychological Interpretation of William Blake*] offers many insights into the undoubted archetypal contents of Blake's mythical poetry, if the reader does not insist on academic prejudices about scholarly sources and causal argument. . . . ''

From a reading of Van Meurs's wide-ranging survey, one sees how much Jungian literary criticism suffers from the same doctrinal obsessions as Freudian literary criticism, and this at a time when "academic" critics seem most concerned with ridding literature of doctrinal or prejudiced readings. Indeed, what still passes for "psychological" criticism here (Freudian or Jungian) seems increasingly quaint. Van Meurs defends the field by saying that "Jungian literary criticism is mostly what has been termed 'expressive criticism', which holds the view that literature expresses the conscious and unconscious mind and feelings of the author, and thereby, in Jungian archetypal view, thoughts and feelings of man and woman in general."

No one denies Expressive Criticism its place, but can it continue to be so oblivious of what several generations of "academic" critics have been addressing as "the text" (as opposed to fantasies of authorial intention)? Van Meurs even draws a battleline for Jungian literary criticism, one that is expressly anti-intellectual: "This means that it is opposed to the more intellectual and abstract pursuits of recent linguistic, structural, post-structural and deconstructionist schools of criticism." He seems to think that what these other schools of criticism do in all their more intellectual and abstract pursuits is somehow not ultimately related to the "thoughts and feelings" of writers or writing, or even related to anything human at all. His confusion comes from believing that only the "psychological" is human and that the other critics are not "psychological" if they don't explicitly discuss certain subjects or take conventional approaches. "Competent Jungian criticism," he concludes pretentiously, "will always belong to that more traditional type of literary analysis and interpretation which focuses on the human content of the texts." Derrida, you alien! (CB)

Klossowski de Rola, Stanislas. *The Golden Game: Alchemical Engravings of the Seventeenth Century*. New York: George Braziller, 1988. Pp. 320, with 533 illustrations. $45, cloth.

A must for anyone interested in alchemy, Jungian studies, seventeenth-century Europe, or the odd, this collection of alchemical engravings with commentary was assembled by Stanislas Klossowski, who is the son of the artist Balthus and the nephew of the Sadian writer and illustrator Pierre Klossowski. Not only is this work filled with never-before-published alchemical engravings (seductively reproduced), but also its scholarship on alchemy is first-rate.

Klossowski's writing style in dealing with such a dense subject as alchemy is not in the least obtuse or boring and does not become a sacrifice to occult mystification. This is unusual for this genre, as even the late, great Mario Praz was unable to avoid a tedious prose in his book on seventeenth-century emblems. Although *The Golden Game* has the size and beauty to become a never-read (only browsed) coffee-table book, its imagistic weight and curiousness can lead a reader to a mine of insights and pleasures. (JL)

Sutton, Peter, ed. *Dreamings: The Art of Aboriginal Australia.* New York: George Braziller and the Asia Society Galleries, 1988. Pp. 266, with over 300 illustrations and 155 color plates. $45, cloth.

Why do writers on primitive or naive art try to validate and justify their subject by comparing it to modern European artists and movements? Is it because this art is alien to their world, or is it because they secretly question its worth? Nothing reflects insecurity about primitive art more than its measuring against Western modernism. For example, on one page alone in *Dreamings*, Australian Aboriginal art is compared to the work of Jean Dubuffet, the Dadaists, and David Hockney. But Aboriginal art blows Hockney (and the others) right out of the swimming pool.

The writers in this book seem to have forgotten (or, even worse, do not know) that it was primitive Pacific and African art which helped inspire and move modern European artists out from the cloaca of beaux-arts realism and decoration. The primitive eye preceded and influenced the modern and not the other way around. In addition, *Dreamings* is mythologically naive and overly informed by deadened sociology, anthropology, and Freudian sexualism, missing the mystery in the art even though the book is called

Dreamings. And so, sadly, Aboriginal art's vision is not carried here in the words.

In spite of the text's shallowness, the book does provide a good introduction to Aboriginal iconography, and it has a useful if bare biographical section on Aboriginal artists. Also the illustrations are lovely, and the color plates convey the delight and strangeness found in this so-called "primitive" art. Buy this book for the pictures. (JL)

Rodman, Selden. *Where Art is Joy, Haitian Art: The First Forty Years*. New York: Ruggles de Latour, 1988. Pp. 236. $60, cloth.

Nowhere is the mythological more alive today than in polytheistic Haiti. Long governed by psychopaths, its poverty daunting to the rare tourist who will even look, its spiritual life, the vaudou world of the *loas*, decried and suppressed by the Catholic hierarchy, Haiti nonetheless teems in its art with a vitality and imagination unparalleled elsewhere. When the Catholic Bishop of Port-au-Prince refused the offer of Haiti's leading artists to paint murals for the interior of his cathedral in 1948, saying "these artists are devil-worshippers," he was inadvertently acknowledging the amazing ability of Haitian art to break through iconic convention. Selden Rodman was finally able to convince the city's Episcopal Bishop to let the artists do the Cathedral of Trinite, and the resulting blaze of color and iconography is a masterpiece of native church art unlike anything seen since Renaissance Florence. From its beginning in the 1940s with the fabulous paintings of Hector Hippolyte (who the Surrealist poet André Breton once said "painted his dreams only because the transposed spirits of Africa guided his hand") to the most recent painters of the Saint-Soleil group (who had to explain to an enchanted André Malraux that they were not painting the *loas* themselves but "for" them), Haitian art has been a brilliant revelation of contemporary mythic images. This book, superbly illustrated, is surely its definitive presentation. (CB)

Seven Shorts on Architecture

In addition to *Spring*'s traditional subjects, the editors are particularly interested in reviewing books that deal with the natural and built environment, the modern city and its pathology. We want to emphasize how architecture, planning and design should long ago have been seen in relation with the idea of *anima mundi,* or the phenomenon of soul in the world. The following titles are briefly noted as samples of books we have recently received and can recommend from this perspective.

Loyer, Francois. *Paris Nineteenth Century: Architecture and Urbanism*. New York: Abbeville Press, 1988. Pp. 478, illustrated. $85, cloth.

Loyer treats the city of Paris as a character under siege. Under the restored monarchy that followed in reaction to the Revolution of 1848, Baron Von Haussmann cracked open the old medieval city and replaced it with a grand imperial plan, complete with great axial roadways that exploded the old faubourgs. The psyche of the place changed. The conflict helped stimulate urban artists like Manet, Degas and Toulouse-Lautrec into portraying the city as a great stage for the modern. Loyer catches the city in the violent and intentional transition between past and future. (RM)

Vidler, Anthony. *The Writing of the Walls: Architectural Theory in the Late Enlightenment*. New York: Princeton Architectural Press, 1987. Pp. 230, illustrated. $35, cloth.

Vidler discusses post-revolutionary architecture and its struggle with the language of neo-classicism as architects like Boullee, Ledoux and Lequeu attempted to invent radical building types and forms to reinforce the revolution's notion of the new man and woman. An architecture free of the old iconographies sustained by former authoritarian regimes proved difficult to effect in practice. Vidler raises issues of authority that have implications beyond his immediate subject and point to the problems of imagining the world outside of the established and decayed hierarchies. Note also in this regard Vidler's edited edition *L'Architecture de C.N. Le Doux* (Princeton Architectural Press, 1983). (RM)

Siry, Joseph. *Carson Pirie Scott: Louis Sullivan and the Chicago Department Store*. Chicago: The University of Chicago Press, 1989. Pp. 290, illustrated. $27.50, cloth.

This book details the development of State Street, Chicago's principal commercial street after the Great Fire of 1871, through Louis Sullivan's steel-framed store for Schlesinger and Mayer. The store was the architect's last major urban building. It represents a belief in the modern severely eroded after the rush by most professional architects to a safer neo-classicism like that practiced in Chicago at the World's Columbian Exposition (1893). Sullivan made himself extinct by continuing to press ahead with an architecture that he chose to view as both inventive and "democratic." As a fantasy, the department store was the perfect middle ground for him between the philistine commercial tower and the vitality of the city street. (RM)

Twombly, Robert, ed. *Louis Sullivan: The Public Papers*. Chicago: The University of Chicago Press, 1988. Pp. 255. $29.95, cloth.

The editor has selected all of Sullivan's major public papers. Read together they provide a view of a romantic artist at odds with architecture's growing professionalism and increasingly antagonistic to the dominant commercial culture of his day. These papers also offer considerable insight into modern self-mythologizing, the process by which an artist begins self-destructively to hyperbolize his own role as heroic and tragic. (RM)

Wagner, Otto. *Modern Architecture*. Tr. and ed. Harry Francis Mallgrave, Santa Monica: Getty Center Publications, 1988. Pp. 185, illustrated. $29.95, cloth.

With this book, the Getty Center begins its ambitious program of publishing critical documents in the history of art and the humanities. Relying on the 1902 edition, with supplementary material from three others, including 1914, this work gives us a close view of Wagner as theoretician and practitioner during the Viennese Secession and later during the formative phase of European modernism. The book is beautifully produced and imaginatively edited. Read along with other modernists like Adolph Loos, who in a famous manifesto called ornament criminal, Wagner's intentions, in his own words, can be seen in a larger political and social environment where all notions of order and inherited culture were being questioned. (RM)

Robinson, Cervin and Joel Herschman. *Architecture Transformed: A History of the Photography of Buildings from 1839 to the Present*. Cambridge: MIT Press, 1987. Pp. 203, illustrated. $50, cloth.

A study of architecture and architectural imagery through photography. The authors discuss developing techniques of architectural photography and provide a way to think about the two-dimensional representation of three-dimensional objects. Placement of the photographer, angle of the view and manipulations of the negative are a few of the ways the world of objects is transformed into what only appears to be a realistic representation, but is in fact an imaginative and heightened form of the "facts." (RM)

Alberti, Leon Battista. *On the Art of Building in Ten Books*. Tr. Joseph Rykwert, Neil Leach, and Robert Tavernor. Cambridge: MIT Press, 1988. Pp. 442, illustrated. $45, cloth.

Written in Latin, Alberti's treatise was the first practical book on the making of architecture since the Romans. A celebrated fifteenth-century work, it precedes the more widely translated and copied work of Palladio which has been used most recently as a model for post-modern architects. It is worth a look at the way Alberti rigorously mines classical forms for contemporary usage. A study of this fundamental text reveals that the rules governing classical architecture were firmly connected to Rennaisance culture. It makes the current appetite for style over form appear nakedly superficial. (RM)

Frantic, directed by Roman Polanski. Warner Bros., 1988.

In this film for the nuclear age, the storyline involves a conspiracy to smuggle out of the United States a high-speed, electronic switch, called a kryton, that can be used to trigger an atomic bomb. Polanski astutely treats this bit of nuclear technology for what it is—a commodity. The kryton is transported by a woman who usually smuggles cocaine. Impersonal forces of demand and profitability propel both commodities along their supply routes, while the film's characters are inadequate to contend with the volatile economics at work. *Frantic* emphasizes the irrelevance of human values to the international trading and use of nuclear technology.

The film takes place in Paris where an American doctor (Harrison Ford) and his wife (Betty Buckley) have flown in for a medical conference. At the airport they unwittingly pick up the suitcase containing the stolen kryton. The smugglers kidnap the wife, and Harrison Ford spends the rest of the movie trying to get her back. We sympathize with his unassuming character as he pleads unsuccessfully with the police and the American consulate for help finding his wife. Two or three times he telephones his children back in America. Two or three times, at awkward moments, he runs into colleagues who greet him with absurd jollity.

But beneath the emotional surface, Arab smugglers of indeterminate nationality, anonymous Israeli agents, and slow-witted American diplomats ruthlessly chase the kryton around Paris. Although each player understands the reasons for his actions and, perhaps, has even weighed the moral costs, none of it matters. Nor does it matter whether the Arabs are middlemen or acting for their own government.

Are the Israelis simply trying to keep the kryton out of Arab hands; are they trying to get it for Israel; or are they "probably on our side," as the American security officer explains? Motives do not matter, yet everyone looks for a human rationale. Harrison Ford discovers that the "White Lady," which a Jamaican dealer offers him in a bar, is not his wife but cocaine. The security officer thinks that she cannot have been kidnapped but must have run off with another man. At least half the movie goes by before the identity of what is being smuggled is revealed. Then, two attempts to make a simple exchange of kryton for wife end with sudden violence. Nobody can catch up to commodity.

With characters as set forth in *Frantic*, Polanski is trying to match commerce for speed and neutrality. His characters are nameless and unrestricted by any of the artist's humanistic handle on things. *Frantic* does not over-dramatize the dangers of nuclear war and is not an especially dark vision of the world. Still, in an era of nuclear proliferation, it should rid us of our disturbing belief in the efficacy of free will and responsibility. (EP)

CONTRIBUTORS

Kenneth Lincoln grew up in northwest Nebraska and for twenty years has taught contemporary and American Indian literatures at UCLA. He has published a study of American Indian writing, *Native American Renaissance* (University of California, 1983), and an ethnographic travel narrative on contemporary Indian life, *The Good Red Road: Passages into Native America* (Harper & Row, 1987). He is presently writing a book on American Indian humor.

Peter Bishop has lectured at the South Australian College for Advanced Education for over eleven years. Previous papers have appeared in *Spring 1981, 1984, 1986, 1987, 1988,* and his book *The Myth of Shangri-La (Tibet, Travel Writing and the Western Creation of Sacred Landscape)* is forthcoming from Athlone (London) and the University of California.

Judith Gleason is a psychotherapist with a Jungian orientation in private practice in New York City. For the last twenty years she has been doing research on traditional African religions in West Africa and the Caribbean. Her latest book *Oya: In Praise of the Goddess* was published by Shambhala (Boston) in 1987.

James Hillman's paper was first delivered as a lecture at the Convegno of the Associazione Italiana per lo Studio della Psicologia Analitica, in Rome, 3 November 1988, and first published in an Italian translation. Response to it by Bianca Garufi appears in *Itinerari del Pensiero Junghiano* (edited by Paolo Aite and Aldo Carotenuto); other responses (in German) by Adolf Guggenbühl-Craig, Niel Micklem, and Mario Jacoby were published in *Gorgo* 16 (1989).

Enrique Pardo, actor and theater director, has published articles in *Spring 1984* and *1988* on theater and archetypal psychology. He is based in France, at Château de Malérargues and, with the Pantheatre/ Enrique Pardo Company, is currently exploring "The Alchemical Theatre" in international seminars and performances. This article is extracted from a lecture given at "The Second Annual Conference of the London Convivium for Archetypal Studies and the Arts," London, June 1988.

Cynthia J. Fuchs is an Assistant Professor of Film Studies at George Mason University, Virginia.

Jay Livernois is a lecturer and doctoral candidate in Comparative Literature at the University of Connecticut. He is presently working on a book titled *The Puritan Woman*.

Morton Smith, with degrees from Harvard University, Harvard Divinity School, and Hebrew University, Jerusalem, has taught at Brown University and, since 1957, at Columbia University, in Ancient History.

David L. Miller is the Watson-Ledden Professor of Religion at Syracuse University. He is the author of *The New Polytheism, Three Faces of God,* and *Hells and Holy Ghosts*.

A. Vernon Woodworth is an architect and a diploma candidate at the C. G. Jung Institute—Boston, with practices, respectively, in Milton and Cambridge, Massachusetts. He is concerned with renovation, restoration, and renewal, both inner and outer.

A principal in Tigerman McCurry and a Fellow of the American Institute of Architects, **Stanley Tigerman** has been a visiting professor at numerous universities and is currently the Director of the School of Architecture at the University of Illinois at Chicago. He has written extensively for architectural journals and has authored several books, most recently, *The Architecture of Exile* (Rizzoli, 1988). He is currently working on his next book, *Failed Attempts at Healing an Irreparable Wound*.

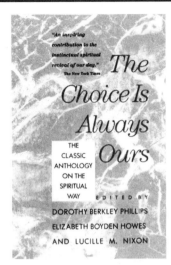

Robert Johnson & Marion Woodman

Homesick for myself, for her— as, after the heat wave breaks, the clear tones of the world manifest . . . a whole new poetry beginning here.

ADRIENNE RICH

femininity

A landmark conference November 11 & 12 in Santa Barbara, California

THE CONFERENCE

Concepts of **femininity** that may have served us in the past no longer suffice, and new ideas are making themselves felt . . . whether we're ready for them or not. Join renowned Jungian Psychologists **Robert Johnson and Marion Woodman**, two of the great innovative thinkers of our day, as they lecture and engage in dialogue to explore this new **femininity**.

PACIFICA GRADUATE INSTITUTE

This conference is presented in conjunction with Pacifica Graduate Institute's **Ph.D. and M.A.** Degree Programs specializing in **Depth Psychology**. These innovative educational programs combine the study of clinical psychology with the **creative arts, contemporary film, literature, mythology and religion**. Classes meet **one weekend a month** at the Institute's campus in the Santa Barbara foothills and are composed of **students from throughout the United States**.

for information on:

___ Johnson/Woodman Conference, November 11 and 12, 1989

___ Personal Mythology with Sam Keen, September 16/17 in Santa Barbara

___ Summer 1989 Dreamwork Seminars

___ Summer Clinical Training Workshops

___ Ph.D. & M.A. Programs with emphasis in Depth Psychology

name _____

address _____

city _____

state/zip _____

Pacifica Graduate Institute
(formerly the Human Relations Institute)
249 Lambert Road,
Carpinteria, California 93013
telephone: 805-969-3626

S I G O PRESS

Titles—Fall 1989

25 New Chardon Street #8748, Boston MA 01944   508-281-4722

Jungian Psychology and New Age Bestsellers

☐ **The Secret World of Drawings** by Gregg Furth
Foreword by Elisabeth Kübler-Ross
ISBN 4462 256 150pp; 6x9; 80+color illus.   **$16.95**

☐ **Androgyny**   (3rd Edition-Revised)   by June Singer
ISBN 4306 375pp; 6x9; biblio; index.   **$14.95**

☐ **Love's Energies**   by June Singer (December)
ISBN 4519 316pp; 6x9; biblio; index.   **$14.95**

☐ **Striving Towards Wholeness**   by Barbara Hannah
ISBN 4322 320pp; 6x9; biblio.   **$14.95**

☐ **Inner World of Childhood**   by Frances G. Wickes
Introduction by C.G.Jung
ISBN 4527 304pp; 6x9; biblio; index.   **$14.95**

☐ **Inner World of Choice**   by Frances G. Wickes
ISBN 4543 318pp; 6x9; biblio.   **$14.95**

☐ **Inner World of Man**   by Frances G. Wickes
ISBN 4535 352pp; 6x9; 79 illus.   **$14.95**

☐ **Recovering From Incest**   by Evangeline Kane
Foreword by Russell Lockhart
ISBN 442X 288pp; 6x9; illus, biblio.   **$15.95**

☐ **Drugs, Addiction & Initiation**   by Luigi Zoja
Foreword by Adolf Guggenbühl-Craig
ISBN 439X 160pp; 6x9; biblio; index.   **$14.95**

☐ **Encounter with Jung**   by Eugene Rolfe
ISBN 4276 232pp; 6x9; unpub letters & photos. **$14.95**

These and over fifty other outstanding titles on Jungian psychology and related material are available by leading Jungian authors such as Emma Jung, Marie-Louise von Franz, Sheila Moon, Gerhard Adler, and Arnold Mindell. All titles are quality paperbacks and sell well in a broad cross section of bookstores in Psychology, Health, Women's Studies, and New Age sections. This list includes all Coventure titles from London.

SIGO PRESS: ISBN PREFIX 0-93843
*All titles available unless otherwise indicated.   London

T**HAT I AM AN AGENT,** but also a plant; that much that I did not make goes towards making me whatever I shall be praised or blamed for being; that I must constantly choose among competing and apparently incommensurable goods and that circumstances may force me to a position in which I cannot help being false to something or doing some wrong; that an event that simply happens to me may, without my consent, alter my life; that it is equally problematic to entrust one's good to friends, lovers, or country and to try to have a good life without them—all these I take to be not just the material of tragedy, but everyday facts of lived practical reason.

Martha C. Nussbaum
The Fragility of Goodness

I SUSPECT NUSSBAUM'S retrieval of Aristotle at least partly involves an attempt to sustain an ethos sufficient to underwrite the institution we associate with the "liberal project," i.e. an allegedly limited state in service to a social economic order based on exchange relations. To use the phrase "the liberal project," of course, is to put the question in MacIntyre's terms but that has the virtue of reminding us that the social-political question cannot be divorced from the epistemological—i.e. can liberalism survive the acknowledgment that it is a tradition when its epistemological commitments are based on the denial of tradition?

Stanley Hauerwas

A N ARISTOTELIAN SUBLIME is, of course, an anachronism, and the concept might therefore be assumed to be of little relevance to Nussbaum's patient reconstruction of Aristotle's poetic ethics. However, the pathos of tragedy, including Aristotle's description of that pathos, is more ethically ambiguous than Nussbaum's account implies, and theories of tragic sublimity like those of Burke, Kant, and Schiller address this ambiguity by supporting that the discovery and empowerment of an ethical identity is both threatened and facilitated by community.

Allen Dunn

I N NUSSBAUM'S READING of Plato I value her recognition of the importance of the dialogue form (but puzzling her insistence that Plato was the main creator of the austere, unambiguous style of philosophical discourse) and her awareness of how difficult it can be to ascertain what choice between the alternative responses articulated within a dialogue "Plato" wants us to make.

Christine Downing

N USSBAUM ARGUES that Aristotle's remarks about the limitations of the ethical life at the end of the *Nicomachean Ethics* contradict both his earlier acceptance of the dependence of a good life on fortune and his commitment to an "anthropocentric perspective" on the human condition. On the contrary, the limited character of human goodness follows directly from the beliefs about its vulnerability that she derives from Aristotle and urges us to accept.

Bernard Yack

WINTER 1989
A SOUNDINGS SYMPOSIUM ON *THE FRAGILITY OF GOODNESS*

For further information or a subscription write Ralph V. Norman, Editor, SOUNDINGS: AN INTERDISCIPLINARY JOURNAL, 306 Alumni Hall, The University of Tennessee, Knoxville, TN 37996-0530.

U.S. Annual Subscription Rates: Individual $15; Institutional $24. Single Copy: $5. One copy of a double issue: $8.

Pomeroy

Ça lui est égal…il a les numéros
les plus récents de SOUNDINGS.

For that unexpected layover, or *n'importe quelle autre occasion
inattendue,* deconstructionists are finding out what smart academic travellers
have always known.

For twenty years, SOUNDINGS has set the standard among the
quarterlies for rigor and adventure in arts, letters, women's studies, religion
and theology, technology and culture, ethics in the professions, war and
peace, and American culture.

Plus ça change, plus c'est la même chose.

PSYCHOLOGICAL
PERSPECTIVES

Editor: Ernest Lawrence Rossi, Ph.D.

A JOURNAL
OF GLOBAL CONSCIOUSNESS
INTEGRATING PSYCHE
SOUL AND NATURE

———•———

Essays and Reviews by leading thinkers who are expanding the growing edge of consciousness:

Norman Cousins	*Marie-Louise von Franz*	*David Bohm*
Charles Tart	*John Stewart Bell*	*Edward Edinger*
Karl Pribrim	*Laurens van der Post*	*C.A. Meier*
Candace Pert	*Gregory Bateson*	*Arthur Hastings*
Rupert Sheldrake	*Gerhard Adler*	*Russell Tart*
Konrad Lorenz	*Ira Progoff*	*Jean Bolen*

SUBSCRIBE NOW!

1 year: $16.00   2 years: $30.00   3 years $40.00

Foreign delivery: Add $2.00 per year

A Semi-Annual Journal of Jungian Thought

Published by the C.G. Jung Institute of Los Angeles
10349 West Pico Boulevard, Los Angeles, California 90064
213/556-1193

THE CHIRON CLINICAL SERIES

Dreams in Analysis

Edited by
Nathan Schwartz-Salant and Murray Stein

Featured Authors

Edward C. Whitmont
New York

Murray Stein
Chicago

Sylvia Perera
New York

Thomas Kirsch
San Francisco

Caroline Stevens
Chicago

Elie Humbert
Paris

Betty Meador
San Francisco

Lionel Corbett
Chicago

Helmut Barz
Zürich

J. W. T. Redfearn
London

August Cwik
Chicago

To order, write or call:
Chiron Publications
400 Linden Avenue
Wilmette, IL 60091
(312) 256-7551
(800) 397-8109 (orders only)

Shipping charges:
$1.50 for one item
$2.50 for two or more items
$6.00 per book overseas airmail

ISBN 0-933029-20-9 $14.95

Name _____

Address _____

_____

Total _____ (Ill. residents add 7%)

☐ Check enclosed   ☐ Visa/MasterCard

Acct. # _____ Exp. _____

Signature _____

HARVEST

A series of lively articles forms this issue of Harvest vol 35 1989-90
on two main themes - Male, Female and Family dynamics, examined in the light
of religion, mythology and clinical theory, and the creative energies of psyche.
Editor: Joel Ryce-Menuhin

ISSN No. 0266 4771

— —

ORDER FORM
Price with postage & packing: £10.00 sterling, $24 USA obtainable from Harvest
Administration, 37 York Street Chambers, 68-72 York Street, London W1H 1DE

NAME   _____

ADDRESS   _____

_____

Please make cheques payable to APC (Harvest)

The Journal of
ANALYTICAL PSYCHOLOGY

Editor: **Rosemary Gordon**

Associate Editor: **Corinna Peterson**

Consultant Editor: **Judith Hubback**

with the assistance of:

**A. Edwards, D. Davidson, M. Welch,
J.W.T. Redfearn, A. Samuels, B. Wharton** (Review Editor)

The Journal of Analytical Psychology, founded in 1955 under the editorship of Michael Fordham, is sponsored and edited by the Society of Analytical Psychology in London. It is one of the main publications on analytical psychology in the English language.The principal aim of the journal is to disseminate the thoughts, theories, and clinical work of C.G. Jung, as well as the developments of his ideas as they occur and are being worked out in England and in all other countries by analytical psychologists and by those interested in analytical psychology. It also draws on contributions that explore the links of analytical psychology with a range of diverse subjects such as the arts, anthropology, religion, philosophy, biology and physics. The journal thus aims to be a stimulating international and interdisciplinary forum for discussion, comments and debates, but emphasis is laid on collating theory with clinical practice and research.Besides the major articles, the journal includes: comments in relation to papers and points of view published in the journal; short notes that communicate seminal clinical or theoretical ideas which may inspire novel lines of thought and research; correspondence; an extensive review section of books and articles; short summaries of "Books Received"; biographical notes of the authors concerned with each issue of the journal; and a bibliographical list of the *Collected Works of C.G. Jung*.

Published for the Society of Analytical Psychology by Academic Press since 1980.

Publication: **Volume 33, (1988), 4 issues**
Subscription Rate: **£30.00 (U.K.Only)/U.S.$58.00 (Overseas)**

For further subscription details and a free sample copy write to:
**Journals Marketing Department
Harcourt Brace Jovanovich Ltd.
24-28 Oval Road
London NW1 7DX, U.K.**

**Journals Promotion Department
Academic Press Inc.
1250 Sixth Avenue
San Diego, CA 92101, U.S.A.**

LMD/0788/A572

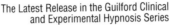

NEW
LITERARY
HISTORY
A JOURNAL OF
THEORY AND
INTERPRETATION

Volume 20, Number 3

Spring 1989

GREIMASSIAN
SEMIOTICS

Ralph Cohen, Editor
University of Virginia

Psychotherapy for Freedom

The Daseinsanalytic Way in Psychology and Psychoanalysis

A Special Issue of *The Humanistic Psychologist*

TO ORDER: Send $12.50 per copy (checks payable to *The Humanistic Psychologist* in U.S. currency) to: Chris Aanstoos, Editor, Psychology Dept., West Georgia College, Carrollton, GA 30118. No charge for postage in U.S., others add $3.00. 1989 subscriptions are available for $10.00 per year (foreign $14.00).